G. W Shinn, H. B Day

The Book of Praise for Sunday Schools

G. W Shinn, H. B Day

The Book of Praise for Sunday Schools

ISBN/EAN: 9783744742269

Printed in Europe, USA, Canada, Australia, Japan

Cover: Foto ©Lupo / pixelio.de

More available books at **www.hansebooks.com**

RELIGION

PHILOSOPHY

&

HISTORY

Four Lectures

BY

THOMAS B. STRONG

BISHOP OF RIPON

OXFORD

AT THE CLARENDON PRESS

1923

PREFACE

THE following lectures were delivered to a mixed audience at Leeds in the early part of this year. By the kindness of the authorities of Leeds University I was granted the use of a lecture-room within the University. For this kindness I wish to express my sincere thanks.

I have revised the Lectures and made some few alterations, but it has seemed better to print them nearly as they were delivered than to expand them into a treatise. I have endeavoured to put forward, in a very fragmentary way, the view that the element in man's effort to interpret the world which expresses itself later as religion is a primary and necessary element in his reaction to his environment; or at least that it has the same kind of claim to validity that is allowed to those elements which express themselves later as philosophy, art, and ethics. At the earliest stage it would appear that these elements are not distinct but fused, and they become separated as reflection grows. For various reasons that aspect of the world which we call science and philosophy comes into great prominence, and endeavours, I think wrongly, to swallow up the others, and to interpret the fundamental ideas of life and ethical action and religion by principles derived from the observation and uniformities in the physical world. The conflict, which is thus apt to arise, is relieved when the world is seen from the point of view of the Christian religion, as an historic process through which God expresses Himself, through natural law and moral right imperfectly and provisionally, through the Incarnation completely and finally. When the fullness of the time came, God actually sent forth His Son.

I add here the titles of a number of books which bear upon the subject. The list is not a bibliography: it contains only a selection of the works to which I have referred in writing the lectures.

History of Religion.
    Pfleiderer, *Religionsphilosophie.*
    Wundt, *Völkerpsychologie. Mythus und Religion* (3 vols.).
    Otto, *Das Heilige.*
    Söderblom, *Das Werden des Gottesglaubens.* (German translation of Swedish book.)
    Robertson Smith, *Religion of the Semites.*
    Frazer, *Golden Bough,* and *Folk-Lore in the Old Testament.*
    Lyall, *Asiatic Studies.*
    Caird, *Evolution of Religion.*
    Jevons, *Introduction to the History of Religion.*
    Webb, *Group-theories of Religion.*
    Fowler, *Religious Experience of the Roman People.*

Greek Philosophy in relation to Religion.
    Burnet, *Greek Philosophy,* Part I. Thales to Plato.
    Caird, *Evolution of Theology in the Greek Philosophers.*
    Inge, *Philosophy of Plotinus.*

Dill, *Roman Society from Nero to Marcus Aurelius.*
Roman Society in the Last Century of the Western
Empire.

Psychology and Philosophy in relation to Religion.
Ward, *Psychological Principles. Naturalism and*
Agnosticism.
McDougall, *Body and Mind.*
Haldane, *Mechanism, Life, and Personality.*
Lloyd-Morgan, *Emergent Evolution.*
Webb, *God and Personality. Personal God and Human*
Life.
Lord Balfour, *Theism or Humanism.*
Pringle-Pattison, *Idea of God.*

I

WE are so accustomed to the presence of the religious interest in thought and life that we are in danger, at times, of overlooking the peculiar character of the fact that it is there. That it is very widely spread throughout the human race cannot be disputed, though it may be impossible to demonstrate that no race has existed without it. However this may be, there is unassailable evidence of its presence to the minds of men from every quarter of the globe, at every stage of progress, and in a most remarkable variety of forms. Perhaps in consequence of its wide range and variety of form, it has proved hard to describe precisely the root-idea of religion, or to account theoretically for its origin and development. Various thinkers have selected some one element, obviously and unmistakably present in most if not in all systems of religion, and have endeavoured to trace from their assumed root the various subsequent manifestations of it. But these various plans have not been successful in making plain the continuity of the earliest and latest stages of the religious impulse. Every one is agreed that the existence of religion raises an important problem, but the proposed solutions of it have not won anything like universal consent. The aim of the present course of Lectures is not to add another to the solutions already before the world, but to consider how the Christian religion stands to the general problem and to inquire what light may thus be thrown upon religion in general and Christianity in particular.

I spoke just now of the peculiarity of the fact that religion is there at all. In every other department of thought the starting-point is in some definite experience reaching the mind, as we say, from the outer world. However lofty and speculative metaphysics may become in the hands of a philosopher, however remote from all our immediate perceptions the principles of mathematics may be or seem to be, they both rest in the end on ordinary verifiable experiences reaching the mind from the outer world. All our intercourse with one another rests upon physical contact of some sort, through gesture and language, or the like. All this is perfectly natural and hardly seems to need explanation: it is so easy to understand how men build gradually out of their physical experiences the idea of a world of sound or sight in which they are perfectly at home, of which they come to know the rules, and which they can use for their own purposes.

But the whole region of religion is different from this. No doubt in some way man, so far as he acts independently in the development of his religion, approaches it from the side of his normal experience. But the result is very different. The metaphysician, however remote and abstract his categories, is still always dealing with the world of sense, and he is expected to show that his principles make experience clearer and more intelligible. His subject and the sphere of his operations is the physical world—interpreted doubtless by the mind, and presented in its universal aspect—but still the physical world. Cause, for instance, is a short name for a certain kind of sequence, of which we have experience. It is not so in the same sense with religion. The main principle of religion—the existence of a God—is not given in the physical world, nor is it verifiable in the same way as other details of experience. Supposing a man has arrived, by whatever process, at the belief in the existence of God, he cannot then walk out into the open air, and say Here or There is God: as he can say Here is the sun, or the ground, or a tree, or a fellow man: or These two physical events are related as cause and effect. It is true, of course, that the philosopher cannot point to his categories existing, as it were, loose in a supercelestial sphere; but he can and is expected to explain how he came by them, in terms of the world of physical experience. The religious idea is more than an explanatory formula or a system of categories, and is not capable of such verification as belongs to these efforts of the philosophical mind. It is then, I think, a peculiar thing and one deserving of consideration that the step towards the religious idea should have been so widely made.

It is easy and natural to find an explanation of this character of the religious impulse in delusion. The reason, it would be argued on this hypothesis, why men have conceived an unverifiable idea of this sort is that they have blundered. Their religious speculation is just a special case of the instinct for explaining which appears in metaphysic, only it is complicated by an anthropomorphic method. Instead of being satisfied with an abstract formula, in which the common nature of a number of experiences may be expressed, religious speculation has conceived the world as created and governed by a being like a man but with many of man's limitations left out: it is idle to look for any serious verification for such an idea. There is truth in this line of argument. It is, no doubt, perfectly true that anthropomorphism enters into man's intellectual treatment of his experience, but I think that this is an inadequate explanation of the religious problem. If we ask why so large a portion of the human race has been led to adopt a belief of this kind, we must search rather farther than this for a complete answer to the problem. Unfortunately it is impossible in a short course of lectures to attempt a complete answer to the question : it may be possible, however, to say something which may point the way to a solution. I shall as far as possible avoid technical language.

We may, perhaps, put our question in this form. Why is it that men have been led so largely to adopt a belief which they cannot verify in the physical order— to mix up with what actually affects the senses, things that, in ordinary phraseology, are not there? A part of the answer to this question—if I may again use rough or untechnical language—is that all intellectual processes of whatever kind are formed by a combination of what is given from outside with what is supplied from within. We often talk—with that freedom from anxiety as to exactitude which is apt to characterize ordinary conversation—as if the mind were like a blank sheet of paper upon which external things wrote down impressions. Such an account of our mental processes, though some philosophers have accepted it, is no longer tenable. No one, I think, would now be found to deny that in the most passive-looking forms of mental achievement, the mind is vigorously active or contributes by its activities to the result. I will try to illustrate what I mean by one or two instances.

Let us suppose, first, that a farmer, a botanist, and a poet are looking over a gate at a field of ripe corn. Can we say they all see the same thing? To this question

we must answer Yes and No. We may perhaps assume—
though it is a bold assumption—that the rays of light
reflected from the corn fall more or less in the same way
on the retina of the three, and excite their optic nerves
in more or less the same way. In this sense the answer
to the question is Yes. But at that stage it would be
rather difficult to say what it is that they see. The
process as thus conceived is purely physical : it can be
exhaustively described, for all I know, in terms of matter
and motion. Let us then go a step farther : they all see
a field of corn, let us say. But then, is that true ? For
ordinary purposes, Yes, but, if we wish to be exact, not
altogether. What they see, assuming it for a moment
to be the same thing, is not *a* field of corn, but that
particular field of corn that is before their eyes. When
they begin to talk of *a* field a great deal has happened.
Various mental processes have been at work. Certain
features of the scene have been noted : these have been
compared with previous similar experiences : a general
idea, built up out of these memories, has been formed,
and the actual scene present then and there has been
related to them as one of a class or type. All our three
observers can use the same words to describe what they
see, but it would be difficult to be sure that, even at
this stage of thought, the associations which enable
them to use the same word are really the same in all
three. No two people have quite the same antecedents
and experience, and it is therefore probable that the
actual contents of their minds may be different even
when they use and understand the same words. This
difference becomes much more pronounced when we go
farther in our consideration of them. I selected as a
suitable trio a farmer, a botanist, and a poet. It is

practically certain that in all the wider and more remote associations of what they saw they would differ profoundly. The farmer might see a crop worth so much a quarter in the market : the botanist might be thinking of genera and species and the classification of vegetables : the poet, if the ears were stirred by the wind, might be reminded of Virgil's lines in his description of Camilla (*Aen.* vii. 808 sqq.).

All this, of course, is the veriest commonplace, though in our hasty way of thinking and talking in ordinary life we are apt to overlook it. I have mentioned it because I want to mark, in the very simplest and apparently obvious operations of our mind, how much more and how much less there is in our thought and speech than we always remember. If I say, I have seen a tree outside, every one knows what I mean. But there is much less in the statement than in the experience which it describes. I saw a particular tree, of a particular genus and species, in a particular place or time, and all these details are left out of my statement. They would make conversation impossible if they were included. I say enough to set the mind of another person floating in normal channels : if he likes he may construct for himself a picture of what I have seen : but my words give no picture. The general term 'tree' is a bare abstract drawn from many individual occasions, and it is very hard to say exactly what it conveys. That is what I mean when I say there is much less in such a statement as that I have been considering than there is in the experience it describes.

But it is also true to say that there is much more. In the background there is all the cloud of memories and similar experiences which enables us to construct an abstract general term. They are not all consciously present, but they are there, and are not ineffective. The mind does not merely register in a passive way the impact of some outer stimulus—to use again ordinary uncritical language—it is active and constructive even in the simple process which we call observation, no less than in its more complex and deliberate efforts. Indeed, we may even say that it is this active element in mental processes which is characteristically human, and which as it grows in range or complexity creates a wider and wider gulf between the mental processes of man and those of his animal brethren. We are tempted, from time to time, to try to distinguish between the real and the work of the mind; but the effort is futile. That there is in every thought an element in regard to which the thinking subject is a receiver is, no doubt, true, and it is useless to endeavour to explain this away; but there is no stage in the evolution of thought at which the thinking subject is a receiver only, and his success in mastering the world depends upon his power to enlarge continually the controlling ideas by which he first understands the world and then comes to bend it, within certain limits, to his will.

So far, I have considered what may be called the mental contribution to the process by which the world becomes known. I may have to recur to this matter later on, but I shall not have time in this course of Lectures to work out in detail the various forms which this mental activity has taken. I will only say here that I include within this idea the more abstract and comprehensive of our regulative notions by which we construe our experience. Space, time, causation, matter, motion, are all of them, as it were, general terms—more com-

prehensive and illuminating than such simple ideas as
that from which we started, viz. the tree, but standing
in an essentially similar relation to the 'given' element,
which they interpret and in some measure control. If
what I have been saying is true, we must recognize in
our attempts to realize the universe of our experience as
a system of fact or truth the presence of an element
which depends upon our mental activity. But we cannot
infer from this the validity of the distinction between
the real and the work of the mind : we should be unaware
of ' the real ', and it could have no meaning for us if it
were not for the work of the mind.

I want now to pass on to the consideration of certain
other aspects of experience, in which also man deals in
an original way with the material that reaches his
senses. In the case which we have just been considering,
his activity is justified by the vast, though probably
limited, control which it gives him over the world in
which he lives. The cases which I am now proposing to
consider lack this verification, or at any rate the conten-
tion that they do is plausible and can be effectively
argued. Man approaches his experience not merely
with the object of finding out what it is in fact, and how
he may deal with the conditions with which he is presented : he also claims to criticize and judge it. This
he does in two main forms. For convenience, I propose
to speak of them separately, but I must not be supposed
to suggest by this that they appeared in the order
I have selected in the course of man's evolution. These
two forms of mental activity are, of course, art and
ethics.

Both these methods of approaching the world start
like that we have been considering with the ordinary

experience of man : and like it again they add something to what they receive. Of the two, art always seems to me the hardest to explain, partly from the difficulty of understanding its origin, and partly because the form of art in which I have most interest, viz. music, has so many special difficulties of its own. I do not propose to attempt a philosophy of art in passing, or to touch upon all its problems. I merely wish to touch upon its position in man's mental structure, avoiding, as far as possible, technical expressions. And I will start at this point.

For some reason or other, from very early times, man seems to have taken pleasure in imitating by drawing or modelling objects such as his early experience supplies to his observation. It is suggested by some thinkers that this pleasure arose from the hope of controlling for his own interest the objects represented ; in other words, they find the roots of artistic representation in magic. For myself, I do not think this explanation is adequate ; it is too simple, and I think underrates the possibilities even of the undeveloped human mind. Any one who has studied the series of Bushmen's Drawings published some years ago could, I think, hardly deny that a very undeveloped race found interest in representing some of the ordinary scenes of their daily life, and it is not easy to see what magical value such representations can have had even to a Bushman. Philosophers exercise great freedom in assigning to infants and undeveloped races conjectural ideas and impulses, but even in this matter freedom should not develop into licence. What seems to be certain is that the instinct leading towards artistic representation began in extremely accurate observation, together with a process of generalization somewhat analogous to that by which we construct general terms. Further, there was something in this impulse which led it away from the line of change followed by the speculative intellect, pure and simple, and caused the disappearance of the desire to control nature by artistic means, if ever that was present in the process at all. The artistic mind not only observes carefully and precisely, and reaches general ideas : it would seem inclined also to improve on its observations—to generalize, but also to idealize. It aims at showing what might be, on the basis of what is : it produces representations which are not merely copies. Minds which are, so to speak, limited to observation will say that the artist combines observed excellences and omits observed defects and so produces his ideal representation. But this again does not appear a sufficient account of the process. It would seem rather that the artist looks at things with a human interest, of truthful accuracy mixed with desire, and that it is this fuller sense of things which distinguishes him from the speculative thinker and accounts for the element of passion which marks art in its highest ranges, and must not be assumed to have been absent from it in the lowest. Opinions may differ as to whether this is a correct or even a tenable view of the function of art in the mental equipment of man ; but I think that if anything of this kind be true, even if the magical origin of the aesthetic instinct be held, we are in presence of a new way of dealing from the side of the thinking subject with the given material. It has some points of resemblance to the method already considered, but it differs at least in one important feature. It is not possible to verify the intuitions, or whatever else we call them, of the artistic mind in the practical ways of life. There is often a very strong contrast between the artistic ideal and the actual experience of life. It is therefore always open to any one who chooses, to treat the artistic conception of the world as pure imagination and to deny it all claim to serious consideration.

So far we have been considering the reaction of man's mind upon his environment: we have thought of his effort at knowing it, and of the way in which he gives it a a human or ideal interest. I must now pass to the very important aspect of things which arises from the criticism of human life as such. We have noted the appearance of what we call, in later and more developed language, the ideal, of the way in which man generalizes and idealizes the result of his observations. When he comes to think of his own life, he brings it and the events considered in relation to it under the distinction between right and wrong—the thing that ought and that ought not to be. There is a considerable advance here from the position of an artistic view of the world. We saw in regard to that the presence of an ideal, i.e. of a view of things and forms which transcended what was exactly observed. But there was nothing in it which precisely required that things should be other than they actually are. The artist who conceives a beautiful form may feel that his artistic sense would be better satisfied if the world were as he conceives it : but he does not feel that things are wrong in the ethical sense, nor does he conceive himself as in any way bound to set them right. When he comes to think of his own life, man is not satisfied to leave either his own actions or those of others exactly as they are : they ought not to be so, he thinks, and he is bound, so far as in him lies, to act on a different plan. This point of view, no doubt, takes many forms, and some of them are very primitive, but the moment is an important one, when man gives this highly humanized tendency to his thoughts about the world. It goes a great deal farther than either of the other points of view which we have considered: the world is seen more definitely and completely in relation to the nature of man: it is realized that his conduct, which may take a variety of forms, contributes to the existing situation, and that he has some power of affecting it for better or worse. Endless questions arise as he works out the meaning and the consequences of this line of thought in his experience: with these we are not now concerned. What concerns us is that when the moral level is reached, man uses a method of interpretation of experience which is comparable to that of the intellect, but involves a more constructive and more independent activity. We noticed that when his object is to find out what is there before him, and to obtain theoretical and practical mastery over the world of observation, he selects, compares, and reduces to abstract shape the experiences which befall him. All this he still does when he reaches the moral level: but he also does much more. He is not content with observing and classifying his experiences; he guides himself also by the idea of a better order, which he and his fellow men have some limited power to create. But his ideal at this stage is also less capable of verification than the other. In spite of many errors and foolish imaginings there can be no doubt that the process which has ended in modern natural science has amply verified itself. It is less certain in the moral world. 'One might mention here,' Bishop Butler cautiously remarks, 'what has often been 'urged with great force, that in general less uneasiness 'and more satisfaction are the natural consequences of a

'virtuous than of a vicious course of life, in the present
'state, as an instance of a moral government established
'in nature; an instance of it, collected from experience
'and present matter of fact' (*Anal.*, Pt. I, ch. 3, p. 50,
ed. Oxford, 1874). But he hastens to add, that 'it
'must be owned a thing of difficulty to weigh and balance
'pleasures and uneasinesses, each among themselves, and
'also against each other, so as to make an estimate, with
'any exactness, of the overplus of happiness on the side
'of virtue' (*ibid.*). There is a startling contrast here
with the success of speculation upon the natural world,
but what is still more important to be noticed is that this
reserved and 'probable' result, which is, perhaps, all that
can be claimed beyond dispute, does not make any
serious difference to man's moral ideas. In spite of set-
backs and disappointments and wrongs of every kind, he
has not had his moral ideal crushed out of him ; and,
though the balance in many virtuous individual lives is
on the side of pain rather than of pleasure, it is certain
that the movement of the race has justified its defiance
of experience. In a variety of ways, by taboos, totem-
laws, and the like, man has, as it were, protected himself
against the danger of giving in too unequivocally to the
mere result of events : he has preserved his sense of real
right and wrong by methods which, later, he has found
to be irrelevant, and has discarded.

A further stage is reached when the world is conceived
as the scene of the presence and activity of a power which
governs the whole. A German philosopher, Dr. Otto, in
a work called *Das Heilige*, has found a convenient
adjective which describes this point of view. He speaks
of a numinous sense : a numinous locality : that is, he
thinks of the mind of man feeling the existence of a

Numen or Presence in a particular place ; and he regards
this sense as the source of the definitely religious view of
things. The word *numen* occurs in Virgil with some
suggestion of this meaning. For instance, *Aen.* iii. 372.
Aeneas has consulted Helenus about his future. Sacrifices
are performed, and Helenus leads him by the hand to the
temple of Phoebus—*multo suspensum numine*—bewil-
dered by the presence of the god in power. This sense
of a presence which Virgil describes thus elaborately is
probably at the root of the religious sense.[1] It would
appear that the sense of such a presence or power created
a feeling of awe, and developed a desire for intercourse
which would necessarily be governed by rules of some
kind. Mr. Fowler emphasizes the presence in connexion
with the word *religio* of ' the feeling which prompts the
cult', and would, I think, imply that the presence of such
feeling is essential to the religious idea. This notion
results in a view of the world which differs in certain
respects from all the others we have considered. The
world is not merely an object for the understanding or a
scene for action, but has in it some life of its own, with
which man's self can enter into relation. This, we may
say, is a new step in the interpretation of the world, and,
as in the previous instances, there is more in the religious
construction than is given in the impact of external
stimuli upon the senses. There is, as it were, life, not
wholly unlike human life, in the world.

The general result of our reflections, so far, is that in all
his mental activities, man is more than a mere passive

[1] Cf. W. W. Fowler, *Religious Experience of the Roman People*,
p. 118.
[2] *Transactions of the Third International Congress of Religions*,
vol. ii, p. 172.

receiver. He certainly gets from outside, to use the ordinary phrase, the material of his mental processes : he works upon a world which he does not create. But he builds up for himself a *Weltanschauung*—a way of looking at his experience which satisfies various expectations in regard to it. And the question necessarily arises, What is the justification for all this original activity? This is really the central question of all speculation : it is really the question whether man can trust his personal powers at all. Within our present limits it is impossible to deal with this problem speculatively or historically. There are certain things, however, which may be said about it.

We have already noted that there is a great distinction between the interpretation of the world as a material system, and the aspect of it as an artistic structure, a moral order, and a mode of divine self-manifestation. The first of these must be assumed, consciously or unconsciously, by every human being who proposes to live an ordinary life. However theoretically sceptical he may be, however ingeniously he speculates upon his experience, for ordinary purposes he must live like other men, and act on the same presumptions as they. Partly in consequence of this fact, and partly from the way in which the phenomena of ordinary experience penetrate all mental activities of whatever kind, it has been attempted to deduce the less obvious aspects of things from this as the original. Art has been traced to observed utilities of various kinds, morality to the complex effect of experience of pleasure and pain, religion to the attempt to reach a First Cause. I venture to think that these efforts, though great names are associated with many of them, and much argument has been expended upon them, are unsatisfactory. In the first place, the imaginary processes by which man is supposed to pass from the observation and co-ordination of definite phenomena, to the conception of systems which are not fully verifiable at all, seem to me unconvincing. There is a real gap between the observation of pleasant or painful experiences and the most rudimentary idea of right and wrong, and, while it is hard but possible to maintain the faith in a moral order against serious trial in the higher stages of experience, the effort to do so in the earlier conditions of humanity must be continually discouraged. Yet we find that very undeveloped races adhere with extreme tenacity to practices which they regard as right, and take measures to maintain them. They are curious and repulsive to us, but those who follow them see in them a real ethical value, though they do not call it by this name.

Secondly, I am inclined to doubt whether we have really gone the right way to work in the matter. One of the most noticeable features of the mental activity of undeveloped man is myth. There is no doubt whatever that the making and relating of myths is a popular amusement among all savage tribes. And it is true that myths are frequently myths of explanation, supplying some sort of theory of the origin of things, and histories, and ritual. It is therefore not unnatural that a large part of the literature of comparative religion is concerned with the analysis and classification of myths. And it is also not unnatural that as so many myths aim at the explanation of some phenomena, physical or otherwise, there has been a tendency to see in this the primary source of the whole religious impulse. It has been frequently pointed out (by Pfleiderer, Robertson Smith, A. Lang, and others) that this method involves a misconception of the function of myth. Though frequently connected with religious ideas and the current beliefs in gods myths are not necessarily religious at all, and religion appears to display itself in practices, such as prayer, sacrifice, and the like, which are not necessarily connected with myths. I am inclined to deprecate seeking for too articulate an account of the meaning or purpose of the religious impulse in its earliest stages. It goes with all the other ways in which man deals actively with the data of his senses, and when we look at the process from our developed point of view we can trace a variety of interests present in the effort. But I do not think it is possible to say, for instance, that man is first attracted by the problem of causation in its rudimentary form and proceeds to extend his inquiries in various directions from this basis. I would suggest that his thought is really anthropomorphic from the first : at any stage at which he can be said to think he finds something like a reflection of himself in the world around him. He looks to it to satisfy his sense of secure order, of right and wrong, of fellowship. All the special modes of conceiving the world are, as it were, fused : and it is somewhat of an anachronism to treat them in the early stages either as co-ordinate separate interests or as a logical series. As time goes on, and man's mind develops, different aspects of experience catch the attention of different minds. I shall hope to call your attention in the next Lecture to the way in which philosophy separates itself from religion, and different religions lay themselves out, as it were, to satisfy different problems. It is, I think, the response to all of them which is the true and full answer of man's self to the stimulus of his environment, and it is in Christian theology that we find all these various elements resumed after their long independent history.

The desire to avoid technical discussions and side-issues has resulted of necessity in a somewhat dogmatic method of presenting the position. I propose, however, to add here some further remarks upon the main point to which I wish to draw attention, viz. the suggestion that in the earliest stages aspects of man's view of nature are fused which are ultimately treated in separation. Such a view would, doubtless, have presented difficulties to psychologists or logicians in certain stages of the development of their subjects. For many centuries it has been customary to treat the soul as substantially different from the body, as standing over against it, and controlling it from outside. Upon such a hypothesis it is natural to conceive of a central soul exercising various faculties, just as a body exercises various limbs. Every such activity would then be an expression of the central soul or self, and all the thoughts and volitions and other acts are held together by their relation to the central soul. Such a hypothesis also lends itself to sharp logical distinctions between acts of various kinds. Just as man uses his arms and his legs for different purposes, so it might be held that his will is quiescent when he thinks abstractly, while his thought gives direction to the will but is inert and inoperative unless the will carries into effect the ideas of the mind. We are all probably familiar with language such as this : indeed, it has affected our ordinary speech. But more recent psychology has departed from this point of view. It is now clearly shown that thought, even in its most abstract forms, has an element of deliberate and purposive activity in it, and that there is no point at which these two elements are completely in separation. In other words, the sharp division between the speculative and practical elements in man's mental activity is out of date : the two are always combined. If this be true in the later developments of human thought, when the various interests are consciously separated and considered separately and in abstraction, it is the more easy to consider them as fused and hardly separable in their earliest manifestations.[1]

It is, of course, very difficult to conceive the earlier processes by which man justified his existence, so to speak, on the mental level. We are so accustomed to an articulate system of thinking that it is hard to imagine how such a system arose out of inarticulateness. There are two considerations which I venture to think may throw light upon the subject.

(1) All around us we have the animal world, and we enter into relations of considerable intimacy with some animals. Any one who has lived in a house with a clear-headed and determined cat finds himself in contact with something like a system of mixed thought and will. I mention the cat rather than the dog, because its mental system, if we may use such language, seems to me more original and personal than that of the dog. The desire of the dog to share in human life seems to me to lead it, like inferior journalism, to express a rapid opinion upon more subjects than it understands. The cat has its own life, which touches here and there the lives of those human beings with whom it condescends to dwell, but its real life of thought and will, if we may use such phrases, is independent of theirs. Even within its own kind it is individual: you cannot imagine cats hunting in a pack or giving tongue in combination like hounds: the lyric ecstasy of a duet satisfies the social element in its music: *cor ad cor cantat*. We look on and distinguish aspects of its life as we do with our own : but is it not probable that to the cat itself these aspects are fused ? If they

---

[1] Cf. Fowler, *Religious Experience*, p. 227.

were not, it would probably have had to talk about them. And is it not probable also that in the remote and undeveloped age of man, though he may have begun to talk about his experiences, perhaps even may have taken the fateful step towards abstract thinking which will ultimately land his race in metaphysics and theology and mysticism, the various aspects of things are fused? He reacts to his experience as a whole and finds something like himself in it.

(2) Just now I mentioned mysticism : and if, as I think, the numinous sense—to use again Professor Otto's word—forms the element in the feeling of the external world which when separated out becomes religion, the word mysticism is not out of place. But so big a word, one so closely associated with the loftiest achievements of the religious impulse, may seem inappropriate to a state of mind that has by hypothesis barely risen above the animal. I do not think this is a really effective objection, for this reason. When we talk of mysticism we are apt to confine our ideas to its more marked and elaborate manifestations. But this I think is wrong. It is truer to say that mysticism begins when once man has begun to feel something more in his experience than the mere impact of an inanimate world, and I cannot imagine any stage of the human response to the world, however lowly and inarticulate, in which this step has not been taken. Religious experience may be real at all sorts of stages below the highest, and may be created by the simplest things. The poet who wrote the mystical and inspired lines in *Tintern Abbey* also wrote the line—

Spade ! with which Wilkinson hath tilled his lands, and I think he would have deprecated too sharp a division between the degrees of inspiration of the two poems.

II

IN the previous Lecture, I tried to explain what I believe to be the way in which man approaches the world around him. He distinguishes himself from the environment in which he lives, but he claims (unconsciously perhaps in the earlier stages of his development) that he has the right to understand and in some sense control it. In the earlier chapters of Genesis the control of the world is placed in the hands of man: this corresponds in fact with what man actually claims. It is probable that in the earlier stages of his history aspects of the world which we now distinguish sharply were not distinguished, but we can, I think, understand from our own way of dealing with our experience what the elements are which have been present throughout. Let us just consider these, as we know them, for a few moments.

1. We all of us expect to find a rational order in the world around us; that is to say, we expect (for instance) that certain things will always be good for us if we eat them, and certain things will always destroy us if we eat them. Life would be altogether impossible if bread sustained life to-day and destroyed it to-morrow, or if prussic acid destroyed life to-day and sustained it to-morrow. Again, we have, as we say, five senses: we hear and see and touch and taste and smell. That means that objects in the world affect us in various ways. A strawberry appeals to sight, touch, taste, and smell; a trombone reaches us by means of hearing, sight, and if we play it ourselves, touch. The sight of a strawberry is a different thing from its taste, though one may call up the other. But in spite of these differences we always behave as if the

world to which our various senses introduce us were one and the same world. Unless we can believe that the world around us is a single system, upon the rules of which we can count, we cannot think or act in it at all.

2. We do more than simply observe and co-ordinate facts ; we also deal with what might be or ought to be. And when we reflect upon our life in this light we feel a demand resting upon us to guide our actions in accordance with our ideal. And we believe that ultimately the facts of human experience must conform to our ideal—though it may involve a long and tortuous history before this end is reached. There is an ideal of right as well as an ideal of order.

3. We are not content to regard ourselves as living in a dead world : we look to find in it some kind of presence with which we can get into fellowship. Some process like our own thought and action must underlie the world we know if it is to be rational in the full sense, and to justify our expectations.

4. There is no intrinsic reason why these last two expectations of the world around us should be less valid or less likely to be satisfied than the expectation of regular order. We come at them in similar ways and they are necessary to the confirmation of our ethical and religious instincts. There is, however, a difference in one important respect. If the physical world is not orderly, our physical life cannot go on. But our ethical and religious life can go on, though our ethical and religious ideas are very far from complete realization. No doubt, in the end, the total failure of the ethical ideal would mean the total failure of human society and a fall into and beyond barbarism. The total failure of the religious hope would mean a failure of the ethical ideal,

and thus indirectly the collapse of humanity. But whereas the failure of the physical ideal of order would mean instant disaster, the failure of the other ideals would or might produce its results more gradually.

I contended in the previous Lecture that these aspects of the world are inextricably interwoven—that the complete response of man's mind to his environment includes them all, and that, so far as can be seen, they are not sharply distinguished in the early efforts of thought. As things go on, distinctions become possible. Different minds are attracted by different elements in the whole situation, and hence arise separate and distinct methods of systematizing experience. I wish to speak to-day, first, of that which has occupied perhaps the largest space in the history of thought, the growth of scientific or philosophical knowledge, and then of certain special developments in regard to religion.

Every one, as I noted in my previous Lecture, starts with the world before him, and his life consists very largely in the effort to control it and use it for his own purposes. Now the world, as the child in Stevenson's poem observes, is full of 'lots of things' : and though we ought in consequence to be 'all as happy as kings', that is not possible unless we can discover some way of understanding our world. What we want most, perhaps, for this purpose is a sense of confidence and certainty : we want to be able to count on events happening in a certain order and under certain rules, for, if we cannot do this, it becomes altogether impossible to live in the world. We all of us know the truth of this, through our own experience or from what we have heard from other people. We can easily understand, for instance, how terrifying the effect on the mind must be of a bad earthquake, because everything that we are accustomed to think solid and trustworthy is upset. We can hardly have failed to notice that a time of war—especially such a devastating war as that through which we have just passed—creates an upheaval in people's minds even though they are not immediately within the range of the military operations. I remember noticing during the South African War, and it was still more obvious in the late times, that people seemed ready to believe any nonsense that any one thought fit to tell them. We laugh now at the rumours of the Russian reinforcements: we have learnt to hold a more reasonable view than was possible in war-time of the extent and the efficiency of the German spy-system. But in war-time the foundations of our whole sense of orderly trustworthy life were broken up, and stories obtained vogue that would not have attracted any serious attention apart from the War, and that no one has thought it worth while to refute since. In times of great upheaval, physical or moral or social, the mind is demoralized and shaken: 'fear', as the author of the Book of Wisdom says (xvii. 12), 'fear is nothing else but a surrender of the succours which reason offereth': so when men are afraid, they lose control both of their own reason and of their estimate of the world. If we may take the condition of savage peoples at the present day as representative of a stage in the upward growth of all men, we can see in them a picture of life before the realization of its order had come into full consciousness. They are always without the confidence and certainty which civilized men partly lose in times of great disturbance.

Greek philosophy is, for all Western civilization, the most important element in the conscious realization of the necessity of rational order in the world of experience. And this gives Greek philosophy, I may say in passing, a permanent value for all whose speculations, like our own, rise ultimately out of Greek philosophy. Apart from the fact that in Plato philosophical discussion attained the most perfect literary expression, the method of asking the questions and providing the answers has necessarily affected subsequent developments, and it is important to bear this in mind. We have not only to understand and carry on their lines of thought, but also to be mindful of the limits imposed by their time and conditions.

Now the thing which attracted and vexed the Greek mind was confusion and uncertainty : they wanted precision and order, and they sought to attain their end by searching for some one principle which would explain the whole mass of miscellaneous experiences which crowded in upon them on all sides. This search for order took various forms. There was confusion in the current notions of the gods, and if Professor G. Murray is right the religion of the Olympian gods was an attempt at religious reform—a reduction in numbers, and a conception of more or less ordered divine life. It remained, however, that the gods resembled a human society with human passions, possessing greater power, but not conspicuously greater wisdom. In other words, the reform failed, and certain thinkers, notably Xenophanes, a philosophical poet of the sixth century B.C., perceived this. He maintained that there is but one god, supreme among both gods and men, not like mortals either in form or thought,[1] and he explained the development

---

[1] Εἷς θεός, ἔν τε θεοῖσι καὶ ἀνθρώποισι μέγιστος, | οὔ τι δέμας θνητοῖσιν ὁμοίιος οὐδὲ νόημα, Clem. Alex. *Strom.* v. 109.

of the popular view as a piece of anthropomorphism, to use our modern phrase.[1]

Together with this form of monotheism, Xenophanes appears to have held some kind of pantheistic notion of the unity of all existence. That is to say, he began to make religion serve the purposes of philosophy. He began to think of God as the ground of all finite existence, but our knowledge of his views depends on fragments of his writings preserved by later authors, or references to his theories in Plato and Aristotle or others.

There is little difficulty, however, in realizing the monism of the physical philosophers of Ionia. They sought for the unity of things in a development of some primary form of matter, giving various accounts of the way in which the primary matter expressed itself in the multiformity of the world. We need not dwell upon these: I mention them to indicate that the hope of finding a single material basis for things was not ignored. We come to a different stage in thought when we find that reflection upon thought itself governed philosophical discussion. We may begin our consideration of this stage with a few words about Socrates.

It is, as you know, a matter of controversy what exactly the philosophy of Socrates was, if, indeed, he can be said to have had any philosophy. It is, I think, difficult to understand the effect he has had upon the history of thought, if, as has been recently maintained, he held no distinctive views of any kind, and we may perhaps trust Aristotle so far as to believe him when he says that Socrates 'for the first time concentrated thought

---

[1] 'Ἀλλ' εἴ τοι χεῖράς γ' εἶχον βόες ἠὲ λέοντες, | ἢ γράψαι χείρεσσι καὶ ἔργα τελεῖν ἅπερ ἄνδρες, | ἵπποι μέν θ' ἵπποισι, βόες δέ τε βουσὶν ὁμοίας, καί κε θεῶν ἰδέας ἔγραφον καὶ σώματ' ἐποίουν | τοιαῦθ' οἱόνπερ καὶτοὶ δέμας εἶχον ὁμοῖον, Clem. Alex. *Strom.* v. 109. 3.

upon definitions ' (*Met.* A. vi. 3). This harmonizes with the procedure ascribed to him in what are called the Socratic Dialogues of Plato. He continually presses for a definition or phrase which will apply to all the actual cases covered by a term. In the *Charmides*, for instance, he tries to define Courage : and endeavours, in a sanguine mood, to extract a formal definition of it from a general. The general, and in this dialogue his attitude is curiously modern, knows perfectly well what orders to give in a battle, but fails altogether to explain why a particular course of action is described as courageous, and why actions of very different character may be sometimes called courageous and sometimes not. How far the historical Socrates carried out this line of thinking, I leave to the controversial learned : the principle involved is of the highest importance. It means that you cannot really master intellectually the confused mass of your experience, until you can group and classify, and use general ideas. In England we are suspicious of general ideas, and we should probably urge that a practical man like the general above mentioned ought not to be too much worried about theories, and that he would do quite as well without. Plato, at any rate, would have admitted this, but he would have said, as he does say in the *Meno*, that may be true ; a man can do very well if he has been brought up with good opinions : but opinion has, as it were, no real foundation, unless you can find out the universal law which justifies it : only the man who knows that is really secure.[1] Mere opinion is always really confused, like the blurred image of a real thing, and it is only the knowledge of the universal which admits you to certain and changeless reality.

Socrates, Aristotle tells us in the passage I quoted

[1] *Meno*, p. 97 e.

above, was concerned with ethical matters, and not at all
with nature as a whole; suppose, however, this search
for general principles were applied to nature as a whole,
what would happen then? The subsequent history of
Greek philosophy gives an answer to that question.

When we look out upon nature we become aware of a
number of persons like ourselves, a variety of animals, a
variety of inanimate things: if we wish to think of all
these elements of experience we require general terms.
But there are also sequences of events, actions which lead
to results, relations of all sorts and kinds. If we try to
find the general aspect of these we tend to reach a system
of universal laws. In Aristotle's language the only way
of knowing nature is by knowing the causes of things.
He therefore goes farther than Plato at the stage we
have been considering. He understands the difference
between opinion and scientific knowledge, but he gives it
a more precise expression. The man of mere experience
knows as a mere fact what may be true and valuable; the
man of science, ἐπιστήμη, knows why it is true and
valuable: he knows the cause. It is by means of this
knowledge of causes and sequences that man wins his
mastery over the world. If he could raise his knowledge
of these things to absolute completeness he would have
before him the whole course of nature, seen as a complex
of universal laws or principles. The changing details
would all be accounted for, and man's desire for complete
knowledge of the world would be satisfied.

It must be admitted that this ideal of completely
articulate knowledge, though I think it represents the
conception of scientific attainment which would result
from principles which he certainly expounds, does not
take shape in any of the writings passing under his

name.[1] I think this is due, in part, to the fact that he has never fully decided what to do with the individual, and in this he has been followed by the majority of his successors: the proper position of the individual is, and has always been, a trouble to philosophy. I shall have to return to this point again.

If we inquire into the theology of Aristotle there are again two elements to be distinguished. He speaks sometimes of 'the gods' using current phraseology, and in *Eth*. I. ix he even characterizes the view that they have no interest in human life and fortunes as λίαν ἄφιλον. At the end of the *Ethics*, however, he uses more abstract language and affirms that the activity of the gods consists in θεωρία (contemplation). But there is also the purely philosophical aspect of his theological thought. In this mood he drops the mythological language altogether. God is the one source of all motion, and in this sense is, as we should say, a necessity of thought. The nature of His life is perpetual contemplation (νόησις), that is, reflection upon the highest and most changeless object, which is thought itself. To this ideal condition men attain imperfectly for a time. 'If ' then God is always in that good state in which we some- ' times are, this compels our wonder: and if in a better, ' this compels it yet more. And God is in a better state. ' And life also belongs to God ; for the actuality of ' thought is life, and God is that actuality: and God's ' essential actuality is life most good and eternal. We say ' therefore that God is a living being, eternal, most good, ' so that life and duration continuous and eternal belong to ' God: for this is God.' [2]

[1] Cf. Joachim, *Aristotle on Coming-to-be and Passing-away*, pp. xxii–xxviii.   [2] *Met*. A. xii, ch. 7, Ross's translation.

Doubtless this may seem a somewhat remote and unattractive conception of God, even though in this chapter where he is speaking of the way in which God sets up the notion which is the cause of the world-process, he says κινεῖ ὡς ἐρώμενον—he causes 'motion by being loved' (or desired), 'and by that which it moves, it moves all other things'. There is in this phrase, as it were, a survival of religious feeling and emotion, but the theory as a whole is obviously derived from the analysis of experience : it is the final outcome of the original interest in form, and the universal element in things as opposed to the particular. I have already noted a point at which I think the difficulty caused by the individual and particular aspect of experience makes itself felt : in the magnificence of Aristotle's final statement of his theology we become conscious of this trouble again. For as we think of the life of self-contemplation eternal and change-less which is the life of the first Cause, it is clear that we are only a step or two from a pantheism, in which the relation of God and the world are permanent and change-less, and in which the history and the fortunes of mankind tend to become uninteresting and unreal. I do not think that Aristotle ever quite took this step, partly because his strong interest as an observer and practical thinker in the regions of ethics and sociology kept him close to details and facts, and prevented his really facing the question of the degree of reality assignable to the particular events of which our lives are full. But I would also urge that so soon as it is agreed that the universal element in our knowledge is superior in truth and reality to the individual, then we cannot stop short of imagining in one form or another a system of eternal and immutable ideas eternally present in the mind of God and no less necessary to the completeness of His existence than He is to theirs.

I have dwelt upon this philosophy somewhat long because of its enormous importance in the history of thought. Over and over again the effort towards unity of principle in things has led to this result. There are various forms which the tendency may take. The simplest is, perhaps, to regard the whole of human experience as an illusion, and the events and lives in it like meaningless bubbles on a stream without known source or end. This point of view has never made large way in the West. What is more common is a system of pantheism, and how many of our speculative philosophies take this form. The world is conceived as a closed process within which changes take place, but which has as a whole neither beginning nor end : if there is a God, He is in permanent relation with it. The Stoic process from ἐκπύρωσις to ἐκπύρωσις under the dominion of destiny is of this kind : H. Spencer's scheme of a process from indefinite incoherent homogeneity through definite coherent heterogeneity—through evolution, equilibration, and dissolution back to homogeneity again—is closely parallel in ultimate form to that of the Stoics. Many similar systems might be referred to. What they all have in common, as it seems to me, is that they find truth and reality in the general or universal or abstract thought, and that in so doing they lose hold on individual life and on all really new activity and real change. An illustration will show in some measure what I mean. Take the sunrise of to-day. In one aspect, as it meets the eye of any one who may have seen it, it is as distinct from all other sunrises as to-day's *Yorkshire Post* from all other issues. But we have learnt to look at the rising of the sun from so abstract a view, that we now say it is merely an illustration of a fixed law—an inevitable incident in the internal motions of a rigid system of the universe; from this point of view any details that might interest you or me do not matter, and are as if they never existed. If we knew enough about them and took trouble enough we might put them all down under some general rule or other. At present we cannot talk in this way about the *Yorkshire Post*: regular as it is, there were days when it came out in a type-written form, and no two numbers are ever nearly alike. But the ideal of the system of thought which I have in mind would be to bring the *Yorkshire Post* as completely as the planets under the dominion of fixed law. When all things can be fully reduced to the terms of matter and motion, then the person who knows the rules will be able to write history from beforehand, putting all details exactly in their place in a closed and self-contained system.

It is natural that such an ideal, which is really only the complete and logical outcome of the attitude to things of the discursive intellect, should be formed and should guide the aspirations of investigators. It never has been fulfilled, and I think we may add never will be, because it is never really adequate to the experience from which it starts. In the previous Lecture I pointed out that in such a simple phrase as ' I see a tree ' there has been the deliberate neglect of certain elements of perception, and the inclusion, more or less deliberate, of memories and elements of various kinds. These neglected elements are all part of man's experience, and they affect his action as well as his thought; in ordinary intercourse we correct our abstractions almost without thinking about it ; when we come to the widest and supreme abstractions we are apt to forget that any correction is necessary, and of this much confusion comes. It is because of this uncorrected following of a limited and abstract view that the pantheistic theologies, in which philosophy so often ends, are unsatisfying.

We have now considered in outline the independent development of the impulse towards exact and scientific truth. I must now ask you to consider with me the specific development of the religious element in man's conception of his world. I described this religious sense in my previous lecture as a perception of a presence, somewhat analogous to the human soul, with which the human soul desires intercourse. In speaking of the religious factor in man's mental activities, I called attention to the fact that the sense of a presence implies or produces a feeling of the nearness of some being or influence producing awe. Mr. Warde Fowler, in the passage I referred to,[1] quotes a passage from Cicero *De Inventione*, which expresses the meaning of the word *religio*. The feeling leads to a desire for intercourse, and so prompts 'the discovery of the proper rites by which the object of that feeling may be propitiated'. The feeling is not a mere feeling leading no farther; it suggests certain lines of activity. If the feeling were merely a sense of the existence of a being or influence, and led to no desire for companionship and intercourse, it might end in a mythology or a theory of creation or the like, and pass ultimately into philosophy, as much Greek religion did. But the notion that the being in question may be approached in certain fashions and not in others connects the idea sooner or later with morality ;

[1] *Transactions of the Third International Congress of Religions*, vol. ii, p. 172.

this will mean a different process of development. If at first the deity is conceived as having his likes and dislikes, as supporting his friends and damaging his enemies, or even ' Loving not, hating not, just choosing so', the time will come when these capricious likes and dislikes will be connected with the notions of right and wrong—of the world as an ethical system. The influence and interest of the divine power will be assumed to be on the side of right, even when it might be possible to do wrong successfully and without being found out.[1]

This connexion of the religious sense with morality— as the oracle just mentioned proves—is one of the links which binds the idea of immortality to religion. The world as it stands is far from satisfactory to the moral judgement. Evil frequently triumphs over good, and wrongdoing is frequently successful ; there seems to be no way of satisfying the claims of virtue in this life. The conviction of the truth of this drove men to conceive of another world in which such injustice was remedied. Even if wrong gained the mastery in this world, it might be hoped that the man who had failed in this world might be rewarded elsewhere, and that, at any rate, the wrongdoer would be severely punished.

There are, however, two points arising out of it which it is important to deal with briefly. I have called your attention to three elements connected with the religious idea : the sense of intercourse, cult, worship ; the idea of a divine interest in justice ; and the closely allied idea of immortality. In the previous lecture I referred to the fact that one of the first movements in the intellectual growth of Greece was the criticism of the prevailing mythology.

[1] Cf. the answer given to Glaucus, son of Epicydes, in Herodotus, vi. 86.

It was assailed as intrinsically inferior to the moral standard of Greece, and as the result of anthropomorphism a half-scientific, half-metaphysical analysis of the physical world took its place. As Aristophanes says (*Nub.*828), Δῖνος βασιλεύει τὸν Δί᾽ ἐξεληλακώς. And by way of result of this, as the conservatives complained, religious worship was undermined. So, further, moral virtue tended to be withdrawn from the purview of religion. It was no longer necessary to search for divine sanctions for right action, ordinary reflection upon life would show the intrinsic superiority of virtue over vice. The true nature of man would be realized in a life of virtue, and its whole balance would be destroyed by vice. Moral philosophy came to be part of the rational analysis of experience. And then, once more, the question of immortality took on a new colour. The gods were expected to see after the righteous man in the next world, all the more if they had neglected his interests here. But a further question might be raised. It might be asked whether, after all, the soul was not in itself immortal, whether it did not differ in essence and nature from the body, whether the imperfection and weakness and wrong under which men suffer was not just due to this, that the soul through some misadventure had lost its proper state and fallen into prison in the material world.

It will be obvious from this short account that the special religious elements virtually disappeared ; they lost all distinctive character and were merged in the philosophy of the world and the mind. The mythological view of the world as the work of divine powers had given place to something like a mechanical system of law, and had taken with it, for all the educated and thoughtful, all practical religious activity. Moral life, as I have just noted, was covered by practical philosophy; immortality had become a question of the metaphysical character of the soul. Of course, different schools of philosophy took different views of all these questions : there was vigorous discussion in the learned world. There were materialists, as well as idealists; there were hedonists in morals, and people who found their ideal in philosophic calm ; there were those who believed in life after death, and those who thought this life is all; there were those again who doubted the possibility of certainty. Amongst all the thinkers in the various Greek schools there were great men—men who were great in various ways. They stated their problems and formulated their answers in the terms and under the limitations of their age. And there is a unity in the whole achievement of Greek thought. The problems it dealt with were essentially the same throughout, and the theories with which they strove to solve them lay within a definite circle of possible answers. The whole process—from the Ionians to Plotinus, through Plato and Aristotle, the Stoics, Epicureans, and Sceptics —is a history of metaphysical speculation upon certain specific questions, and a limited range of possible answers.

The general result of these considerations is that religion, in any philosophical sense of the word, disappeared as a separate interest; its various problems were taken over by the philosophic schools as part of their analysis of experience. But it is also true that outside this range religious ideas and instincts still prevailed. Ancient religious practices were still kept up, and there was still a recognized religious basis for many social functions. I propose to speak of the Jewish religious development in the next lecture. I have to call attention now to a development which took place at Rome in the last years of the Roman Republic and the early years of the Empire —the spread of Oriental religions in the West.

The religion of ancient Rome is usually described in very unattractive terms, and it is easy to understand its being so estimated. It has none of the brilliance and human interest of the Olympian mythology and is apt to suggest a somewhat sordid conception of life. Mr. Warde Fowler in his important book, *The Religious Experience of the Roman People*, deprecates and also explains this aspect of Román religion. It was, he maintains, truly religious in its earlier forms, it implied a real desire to be on good terms with a supernatural power, and he notes two stages in its historical development. In the first of these, it corresponded to the experience and the needs of the old Roman life of the family ' settled on the land, with its homestead and its regular routine of agricultural process' (*op. cit.*, p. 224). The supernatural powers, of which at an earlier stage little was known, tend to become spirits conceived as living within the bounds of the farm, maintained in friendly temper ' by an orderly round of ' sacrifice and prayer, which is performed daily within the ' house, and within the boundary of the land at certain 'seasons of the year' (*ibid.*). At the next stage, we find in existence an organized religion of the city-state. It has many features in common with the earlier type, but it was the religion ' of the State as a whole, and not of the individual or the family' (*op. cit.*, p. 226). Its rules and details were in the hands of priesthoods, and the individual appears to have been contented to take their instructions. ' In no other ancient State that we know of', says Mr. Fowler, ' did the citizen so entirely resign the regu- ' lation of all his dealings with the State's gods to the ' constituted authorities set over him. His obligatory part

'in the religious ritual of the State was simply *nil*, and
'all his religious duty on days of religious importance
'was to abstain from civil business, to make no disturb-
'ance' (*ibid.*, pp. 226, 227). It is not unnatural to find
that though in many connexions the old private religion
maintained itself, this 'passive obedience', as Mr. Fowler
calls it, 'deadened' the Roman's 'sense of *religio*', that
feeling of awe at the near presence of a supernatural
being which was in him from the first, and so deprived
Roman religion of the power of development, and adjustment to new conditions. When circumstances arose
which required new religious activity, the Romans were
obliged to borrow from other nations—from Greece
perhaps first and then from the peoples of the East.

It was this sterilization of the native religion, through
its law, which explains the great success of the exciting
and enthusiastic cults of the East. This point has been
admirably set forth by M. F. Cumont, in his book *Les
Religions orientales dans l'Empire Romain.* He shows
vividly how the sensuous and entrancing rites charmed
and attracted the Roman citizens in the early days of the
Empire, and how they offered solutions for problems
which the native religion had never succeeded in setting
at rest. They charmed the senses, but they also seemed
to provide profound and ancient wisdom—legends which
could be interpreted to explain the destiny of man and
of the world. They set forth the story of deities which
shared suffering like men, and with whose pain and
recovery the rites would put men into sympathy. Moreover, they promised immortality, freedom from moral
defilement, and a fair passage in the world to come to all
who had acquired their mystic lore. These cults and
the processes in which their ideas were expressed were

successful because they satisfied desires which the old religion had never met, and which Greek philosophy tended to explain away.

Time will not permit me to dwell in detail on this development; indeed, it would not greatly advance my purpose. What is of importance is the fact that in Rome the native growth of religion seemed to be arrested, owing to the stifling influence of the State-religion, and that the reaction from this deadness resulted in the prevalence of those ecstatic forms of worship, which yet did attempt to deal with questions that we have already found stirring in Greek speculation. In the earlier part of this lecture I argued that the definitely religious element in these discussions tended to be lost in the various philosophical systems. It is, of course, true that the cults to which I have just referred retain and intensify religious feeling to the most extravagant degree. But when we look more narrowly at them, it appears that they pass over into, and lose themselves in, the region of ideas. In Book xi of the *Metamorphosis* of Apuleius (born about A.D. 125) there is an elaborate description of the initiation of a man into the mysteries of Isis (cf. Dill, *Roman Society in the Last Century of the Western Empire*, pp. 71-5). The hero of the story, one Lucius, owing to the malign practices of a witch, who handed him the wrong kind of ointment, was turned into an ass instead of a bird (*Met.* iii. 24); he apparently desired to have power at any rate of flying. After many pitiful adventures he at last prays to the goddess Isis, of many names, and is rewarded by a vision of the goddess. He is told to join the procession in her honour on the following day to dedicate a ship as an omen of prosperous seafaring during the year, and to eat a garland of roses which one of her

priests will be carrying. The procession is described at
great length and with much picturesqueness of detail.
He eats the crown of roses: and then 'first the rough
'hair was shed away, then the thick hide grew thin, the
'fat paunch subsided, my feet came through the hoofs
'and ended in toes once more, my hands were feet no
'longer, but were outstretched to perform the acts of man
'that walks erect, my long neck shrank, my face and head
'became round, my huge ears recovered their slenderness
'of old, my strong grinders became tiny human teeth
'once more, and my tail—my chiefest torment—dis-
'appeared' (ch. 13). In consideration of this transforma-
tion he has undertaken to become initiated into the
mysteries of Isis, and the rest of Book xi describes the
process. It is impossible to set this out at length; it
involves meditations and lustrations, secret communica-
tions 'too holy for utterance', and a long fast of ten
days. On the last day, near sunset, in the presence of
others already initiated, the priest leads him to the heart
of the holy place. ' Perchance, eager reader, thou burnest
'to know what then was said, what done. I would tell
'thee were it lawful for me to tell, and thou shouldst
'know all, were it lawful for thee to hear. . . . Yet
'since perchance it is pious craving that vexes thee, I will
'not torment thee by prolongation of thine anguish. I
'drew nigh to the confines of death, I trod the threshold
'of Proserpine, I was borne through all the elements and
'returned to earth again. I saw the sun gleaming with
'bright splendour at dead of night, I approached the gods
'above and the gods below, and worshipped them face to
'face'(ch. 23). He stays for some days near the shrine, and
addresses a long prayer to the goddess in which he sets
forth her control over all the various provinces of being:
the goddess is the principle of life and order in the

universe. After a year he is pressed to undergo another initiation, and submits, though with some protest in regard to expense. And then later on there is a third, as a result of which 'the god that is greatest of the 'mighty gods, and highest of those that be mightiest 'among them, and mightiest of those that be highest, 'and ruler of the mightiest, even Osiris, appeared to me 'in the slumber of the night. To no semblance other 'than his own was he transformed, but deigned to 'welcome me face to face with his own awful voice' (ch. 30).[1] The god recommends him to continue his practice at the bar, and appoints him one of his chief *pastophori*.

I have spoken of Apuleius because, though he is late in date, it is from him that we have the clearest account of what went on in a process of initiation. There is an account, later still, by Prudentius, of the Mithraic rite— the *taurobolium*—which was the process by which a person was initiated into the society of Mithra. Such ceremonies seem strange and savage to us, but I do not think it would be right to assume that they had no religious content in the true sense. They embodied, however crudely, a religious ideal. But attempts to explain them tended to diminish the strictly religious element; the strong interest in finding the philosophical unity in things was apt to predominate over the other. Thus we find Isis appearing as the one force prevailing under many names, and controlling all nature. In like manner the various Gnostic sects in the early centuries of the history of the Church were efforts to use Christian language, modified and adapted, to express philosophical ideas and solve philosophical problems. Like philosophy pure and simple they tended to arrive at religious pantheism.

[1] Eng. Tr. by H. E. Butler.

III

IN the last two lectures I have been considering the position of man in his relation with the world around him, and his various efforts to use it for his own purposes, and to make himself at home in it. We have noted his attempts to find out what is there—the facts and the rules which 'explain' experience. We have noted his attempts to discover the ideal order of his own life, especially in relation to other men; we have noted also the disposition or impulse to find a human or even a personal companionship in the world—to treat it as something more than mere dead matter or a system of mechanical sequences. In the second lecture I drew attention to the immensely preponderant importance given by thinkers of a certain type to the first of these interests, and pointed out that philosophy as it was understood in Greece has claimed for its own ethics, politics, and religion. The three elements in man's response to his environment, which, as I believe, were fused at first, have been distinguished, and one of them—the discursive intellect—has swallowed the others, and claims to impose its methods and conclusions upon them absolutely. I also suggested that this claim usually, indeed, almost necessarily, results in religious pantheism, not by reason of any special taste for this form of religious idea on the part of philosophers, but because their conception of the relation of God and the world is the final form of the desire to reconcile differences in conceptual unity. The mind has gone over the whole of experience, finding general ideas and uniformities, and laws of nature; at the end it resolves the antithesis between God and the world into the eternal relation of interdependent aspects of reality. Neoplatonism endeavoured to get even beyond this, but was then obliged to speak—if I may use somewhat popular language—of the ultimate reality as τὸ μὴ ὄν, the non-existent. Even the Oriental religions which, as I urged, retained certain definitely religious elements, tended to become symbols of theory. I want to-day to urge that Christianity has avoided, at any rate, this peril, and to indicate certain reasons why this has happened.

Behind Christianity lies the history of Hebrew religion, and of this a few words must be said. The whole of this history has been complicated in recent years by the activities of the 'higher critics', and it is not easy to fix dates in consequence. The main outlines of the story are, however, clear enough. There is little doubt, if any, that early Hebrew religion was affected by the religions of neighbouring peoples, and passed through a stage closely resembling those primitive types which we find elsewhere. The influence of Babylon and the Canaanite tribes are said to be traceable in the early stories in Genesis and in the accounts of Israel under the Judges. The Hebrew books themselves represent the ancestors of their own contemporaries as continually attracted by the surrounding forms of heathenism, and continually adopting them. The Captivity and the subsequent experiences of the returned Jews fixed them in the worship of Jehovah. This result was, in fact, the triumph of a particular class of teacher—the prophets— to whom all the neighbouring religions were abhorrent. The majority of modern writers of the critical school tend to throw the date of the actual books late, but it is difficult to believe that the tendency to develop on lines very widely different from those of the nations associated with the Jews does not run far back into their history. Also it is noticeable that in books written according to the critical view late in the history of the nation the memory of highly archaic notions and practices has survived, and I find it, for my own part, rather difficult to believe that the more spiritual aspect of the religion showed no early signs of existence. Fortunately, however, we are not concerned with the dating of documents or the appearance of ideas, and we can confine our attention to points upon which there is widespread agreement.

It is generally observed that the Hebrews showed little or no interest in metaphysical questions. They had no inclination at all to such speculations as those of which I spoke in the previous lecture begun by Socrates and carried on by Plato and Aristotle : the instinct to search into the abstract difference between what is true and what is false in our ordinary experience had hardly any place in their thoughts. Even the question of immortality, which seemed so absorbing to the Greeks, was never a matter of formal debate or discussion. Such belief as they had in a world to come was of the crudest type at first, and owed its changes to the parallel changes in their religious ideas ; it was not a matter of interest apart from these.

The main development of Hebrew religion lay in the direction of a continual growth in the fullness of the personal idea as applied to God. At the earlier stages the God of Israel was not unlike the gods of other nations or tribes; He was a person interested in the people, willing to defend them and maintain their rights. In return for this protection He required religious regards, which continually increased in exclusiveness. As time went on, the tendency to worship, occasionally or permanently, other gods as well as Jehovah, became more and more sharply condemned. The prophets continually connected disaster in the political history of the Hebrews with disloyalty to the God of the Covenant. It became clear that Jehovah was the only true God, and all others were unreal and impotent. Over the whole of this region of Hebrew religion there seems to have been no tendency to reduce the God of Israel to the status of a First Cause, or treat the Divine Being as the logical *prius* of the world. He was clearly recognized as a Person—retaining many traits which we may be inclined to trace back to an earlier anthropomorphic mode of thought—whose character became more definitely understood ; in spite of His severity and the exclusiveness of His claims He attracted the devotion of His people—He was the God of Israel.

The God of Israel was worshipped by sacrifice of various kinds, and an elaborate system of ritual came into being. It is easy to trace in this signs of undeveloped notions of the Divine, and to find points of contact with heathen sacrificial ideas. But in this matter also we find a peculiar line of development. The tribal deity becomes the moral Ruler, without losing His special relation to the Children of Israel ; sacrifice also becomes something more than a mere propitiation, if ever it was limited to this purpose ; it becomes closely associated with moral ideas. The Hebrew prophets developed the sense of sin as distinct from evil : i.e. the idea of wilful transgression as distinct from mere error or lack of knowledge. The wrong they did was from their own will : they did not set it down to ignorance or any other inevitable cause, and for this reason the problem of pain and evil was specially difficult. Punishment for wrongdoing was intelligible enough, but the failure and the misfortune of those against whom no charge of wrongdoing could be laid was a serious and unmanageable question. Further, the process of sacrifice, though clearly required in the divine ordinances, failed to satisfy the conscience or to destroy the tendency to sin. And this would necessarily mean that sacrifice and all other external rites were incapable of restoring a man to the full favour of Jehovah : they failed, unless they carried with them a complete moral reformation. It is not easy to say exactly how all this appeared, in fact, to the minds of the devout. There are passages—e.g. Isa. i—in which the whole ritual system seems to be condemned. I confess I always wonder whether the contrast between outward rites and inward reformation would have taken the same form in pre-Christian Judaism as it does with us. It has to be remembered that the 119th Psalm, if the prevailing view of its date and purpose be accepted, belonged to the worship of the Temple with all its sacrificial adjuncts. The writer, with all his spiritual devotion to the law, and the testimonies and the ordinances, never complains of their externality, or shows any signs of wanting to abolish sacrifice. I am inclined to think that the pious Jew, though he felt the inadequacy of the rites that could never take away sin, acquiesced in them, as God's ordinance. Hence I should doubt whether the last two verses of Ps. li are really incompatible with the unity of the poem.

A further point must be mentioned here. I have already noted that the prophets attributed the many disasters which befell the Hebrews to their constant disloyalty to Jehovah. The evil of the world was, for them, mainly sin, and the result of this expressed itself in the form of political disaster. In this connexion there grew up the notion of a future condition of the people, in which a king, the true representative of Jehovah, should rule over the people in righteousness. Various other ideas came to be associated with this hope. It was one channel by which the Hebrew mind reached the notion of the universal sovereignty of God : when the ideal kingdom was established nations, at present heathen and hostile, would flock into it. In some expositions of this view, especially in the later Apocalypses, the coming of the kingdom of righteousness involved catastrophe— the final destruction of evil and those who were on the side of evil—but the ideal social order which is to come is not sought in a philosophical adjustment of principles but in unswerving loyalty to Jehovah ; it is that which constitutes the ideal order. And the ultimate triumph of Jehovah is made to rest upon the experience of His past action. He brought the people out of Egypt ; He brought back a remnant from Babylon to their own land ; though in consequence of their sin He had dispersed them through the whole world, yet when the time came, He would bring them back. The suffering of the righteous might be explained in this connexion. It was a kingdom to the establishment of which they looked forward ; the process by which it should come would not necessarily be clear to men ; it might ultimately appear that the Servant of Jehovah was smitten for the transgressions of others, and that by his stripes others were healed.

It is difficult to deny that in the Jewish development, which I have indicated so summarily, we have as peculiar and independent a process as that of Greek philosophy. There is in it none of the scientific interest which prevailed in Greece. The Hebrew thinkers are not concerned to find definitions or to interpret their experience by abstract formulae : they conceive the whole order of the world in relation to the personality and activity of Jehovah. In the Greek development, connected, as I argued last time, closely with the search for unity of principle in a confused mass of experiences, the divine element tended to recede, and lose character, and become merely one side of an eternal and necessary relation. There is nothing of this in Hebrew thought, as we have it in the Canonical Books. Their thought develops along the lines of an increasing knowledge of the nature of God. It is the will of Jehovah which history records —His abhorrence of sin, and at the same time His long-suffering. The world is not what it is meant to be, owing to the wilfulness of man : but God's purpose is not broken or thwarted : through all the trouble and mystery of things He will ultimately vindicate Himself.

I must now, at last, come to speak more definitely of the Christian religion, and its relation to what has been said in the previous lectures. If I were setting out a complete account of the Faith in all its aspects, it would be necessary here to say something of present ideas upon the New Testament. There is not time for this, and I will content myself with a very few general remarks.

In the first place, we should notice that the position of the New Testament books as regards authenticity is greatly improved in recent criticism. The very late dates assigned to most of them some fifty years ago no longer hold the field. It would not be true to say that the traditional account of their origin is completely accepted, or anything like it, but there is a strong case for tradition, which perhaps is all that there ever will be in regard to almost all. It will never be easy* to explain the differences between the Synoptic Gospels and that of S. John, or the relations between the Synoptic Gospels themselves. The Acts has gained greatly from the investigations of Sir W. Ramsay ; the fuller and more detailed knowledge he has won of the condition of the cities and provinces in the Roman Empire has led to the explanation of many difficulties. The most widely suspected of the Pauline Epistles are those to Timothy and Titus, and there is wider, but not universal, inclination to accept the authenticity of the others. There are various opinions and doubts about other books in the Canon, especially the smaller ones. For myself, I ought perhaps to say that I think that S. Luke wrote the Third Gospel and the Acts, that the Son of Zebedee wrote the Fourth Gospel and the three Epistles, and, in general, that the traditional account of the books is, in most cases, the simplest and most intelligible. I do not feel sure that any theory, at present known to me, explains the phenomena of the Synoptic Gospels : I am not even certain that the problem of their origin has been stated in the right way. The Apocalypse certainly creates great difficulties as regards authorship, and there are many theories of its origin and character. The most important recent work upon it is that of Dr. Charles, but I am afraid I cannot follow him far in his theories of its authorship and construction.

But, secondly, I do not think that for my present purpose these questions are really of paramount significance, for this reason. The discredit which has fallen upon the late dates once proposed for many of the books drives the ideas contained in them continually farther back. This means that there is less time available for the development of a variety of points of view on the assumed basis of an extremely simple Apostolic teaching, and that it becomes increasingly improbable that the original Gospel was of the extremely simple form which, it seems desirable to some writers to assume. Moreover it was the New Testament, almost, if not exactly as it stands, which has governed the thought of the Church beyond all doubt since the end of the first century. In spite of the various points of view which appear in the various books contained in the Canon, there is a unity in them which accounts for their selection from a number of others, and has fitted the New Testament to be, as it has been, the ruling authority for Christian doctrine until the present day. I propose, therefore, to use the New Testament freely, in the traditional manner, though I shall endeavour to avoid making my argument turn on passages which may be plausibly regarded as containing later developments.

It seems to me beyond doubt that the mission of Christ claimed to be a fulfilment of what had gone before in Judaism. He acts, in other words, with the Old Testament, especially the prophets, behind Him. ' Think not ', He is reported as saying in the Sermon on the Mount, ' that I came to destroy the Law or the prophets : I came not to destroy, but to fulfil ' (Matt. v. 17). ' He sets His interpretation of various precepts of the Law in opposition to that which is current, but He does not claim to have had no antecedents, or to be setting forth a doctrine which His hearers could not be expected to understand. After His mission was over this particular point was emphasized by the first preachers of the Gospel and by

S. Paul. Jesus is in the line of the prophets, but He transcends them all. His coming was a new act on the part of God, marking a new stage in the relation of God with His people; if they could have been induced to see this, their attitude towards the new prophet would have been different. They failed to use the key they had, and by so doing broke the succession between them and the earlier spiritual leaders of their nation. The Church of the first age accepted His claim to fulfil the old Covenant.

The final test of this claim did more than merely verify the claim : it put the whole religious position in a new light. What finally reversed the disaster of the Passion was an event, the Resurrection. This separated our Lord from all His predecessors of the prophetic line : David died and was buried and his tomb was with them at the present time. The Resurrection gave a new meaning to His fulfilment of the past, and marked a new era in the history of men. What is noticeable is that the teaching of our Lord, however it may have prepared the intelligence of His followers for what was to come, was not the immediate cause of the new certainty and joy which they display at the beginning of their evangelical work. S. Paul soon gives a fuller and more elaborate meaning to the message of the Church ; but he also starts from an event or fact, the Resurrection. And in this he sees evidence that a new position had come into existence in the relation of God and man, that some of those promises for which the old fathers had looked were now fulfilled. The dispensation of sacrifice was at an end, because the purpose which the ancient sacrifices figured forth ineffectively had at last been achieved. Through the death and resurrection of Christ, man had become reconciled to God. Thus the whole relation of God and man had changed, and a new power had come to man of living in accordance with the divine will.

It is of importance to notice that in discussing these matters S. Paul does not treat them, so to say, as scientific or metaphysical problems. The Resurrection as he conceives it does not, as it were, add a convincing argument for immortality to a number of inconclusive ones; nor does S. Paul betray any special interest in the problem of mere survival after death. If Socrates had risen from the dead, or even appeared as a ghost to Phaedo and the others who were with him when he died, the arguments which had occupied his last hours would have been relieved of their inconclusive result, and presumably his followers would have been satisfied. But this stands in no relation at all to the attitude of S. Paul, or the early Christians generally. Through their mystical union with the death and resurrection of Christ they felt themselves quickened with new life, over which physical death had no power. Many of them, probably —the First Epistle to the Thessalonians makes it plain— had hoped that for the followers of Christ death would not only have no power, but would never occur again. When Christians began to die like other men, they became nervous. The old vague notion of a doleful, shadowy existence for the dead may probably have revived; was this to be the fate of those who died before the Second Coming? S. Paul assures them that this fear is groundless. Those who survive till the Parousia will not have advantage over those who have fallen asleep in the Lord. Death, though it happens as before, does not separate them from their union with Christ—the Body of Christ of which they are members is one in spite of death.

The Resurrection is an act of God, revealing by the fact that it has happened the truth about man and his sin, and the power and love of God. When this fact is made available for man by his union with Christ, he is a new creature, in S. John's language, born again: he has everlasting life.

It would be possible to work out this teaching of S. Paul into details of various kinds ; I do not propose to do this, though I shall have to touch upon some of the matters concerned in what I now have to say. I have pointed out that the Jewish conception of religion rested upon the belief in a God, who was definitely interested in the world and its history, especially in connexion with the Jews. He was a God of action, who had shown His power and will in certain events of Jewish history. For S. Paul also, God is a God of action, who has shown His power and will in raising Jesus Christ from the dead. I have also tried to show how wide a difference there is between this view of things and that which results from philosophical speculation. Now a system of philosophy, as I tried to show in the second lecture, aims at finding a system of ideas in which all the elements of experience can be classified and co-ordinated. It tends, not from any fault or misconception, but from the necessity of the case, to lose sight of the individual. It breaks him up and, as it were, anatomizes him, and refers his constituent parts to various general laws and ideas. You and I are twentieth-century English people ; our actions, thoughts, even the things we say, are governed by this consideration ; we act, think, and speak as twentieth-century English people must inevitably act, think, and speak. It may not be possible, owing to the incompleteness of our analysis, to explain, as the phrase is, all the life of each of us ; but

the ideal is to do this, and express all our experience in
general forms. But the attitude of S. Paul and of all
Christian thought is not on this line at all. It is as living
agents that they come within the purview of God, so to
speak ; and it is their personal activity in which He is
interested. The Christian position is, in a sense, a comprehensive view of existence—it is a *Weltanschauung*
—but its emphasis is laid upon a different aspect of
human life. Man stands always in a human relation to
God—if we may use the phrase—he is on friendly or
hostile terms ; it is by his actions, day by day, that he
displays his attitude.; it is by His actions that God
expresses His power and will. The basis of all the
Christian view of life is the positive relation between God
and man.

It is true, of course, that in all the Hebrew Scriptures,
and I think also in the New Testament, this point is
expressed in very simple and undeveloped language.
Over a large part of the Old Testament the idea prevails
that a man is affected by the actions of his family and his
tribe. God selects the people, not a number of select
individuals. He lays special commands upon individuals,
but their functions bear on the fortunes of the people. It
is comparatively late in the history of Judaism that the
principle is declared : the soul that sinneth, it shall die.
And even then it is a righteous society—a perfect kingdom—to the founding of which prophets look forward.
So again, S. Paul is intensely conscious of his personal
relations with the risen Lord and the indwelling of the
Holy Spirit, but I do not think he conceives himself as
independent of the Body of Christ, or the Body as an
accidental aggregate of individuals—a secondary product
due to the action of man. I doubt whether this idea of

an individual had yet come into existence, and I think
that much unnecessary confusion has been introduced
into the discussion of Pauline theology by assuming, first,
that he had in view a sort of Lutheran subjectivism, and
then endeavouring to reconcile this with the doctrine of
the Church as the vehicle of God's purpose for the world,
which we find in the Epistle to the Ephesians. Though,
therefore, it is true, as I think, that the basis of all the
Christian view of the world lies in the relations between
men and God, it is also true that these relations are
expressed throughout in terms which the plain man
understands, and that the individual is not conceived as
an atomic unit, but in relation to a corporate life.

It is plain, of course, that a point of view such as this
will be closely concerned with morality. In one aspect
of it morality is a name for that relation between God
and man from which the whole scheme of thought
starts. So we find that God abhors unjust measures, the
oppression of the poor and fatherless, violence and wrong
in every form. And when these things are called sins, it
means more than that they are offences against the law
of the State, or the greatest happiness of the greatest
number, or that they are in contradiction to the true nature
of man. They involve a breach in the true relation with
God ; and they erect an impassable barrier between
them. At this point a number of difficult questions
appear, such as what is later called original sin, but we
cannot discuss them now. The clear result of all is that
religion and morality become most closely connected.
The effort after goodness is an effort to draw near to
God. The failure of human machinery to satisfy the
conscience is more than the pardonable weakness of a
nature prone to error ; it means religious failure, separa-

tion from God, and the apparent failure of God Himself.
To meet this, something more is wanted than an en-
lightened conscience : it is necessary to effect an actual
change : the individual must be transferred from one
environment to another, otherwise the burden of sin
remains.

This again means a different view of morality altogether, a view which is included in S. Paul's antithesis
of the Law and Faith. Before the decisive event of the
Resurrection, the rules of morality appeared, so to speak,
as an external code. The Greek would tell you to
follow a good pattern—such as the φρόνιμος in Aristotle,
the man of sound practical sense. The Jew was con-
fronted by the Law. The Greek might console himself
with the reflection that moral life, though difficult, was
really the most natural form of human existence—κατὰ
φύσιν—the Hebrew moralist might persuade himself
that the Law was the embodiment of the true wisdom,
so that the man who broke it might rightly be called
a fool. But the will was never persuaded by these considerations. When the Law said, Thou shalt not covet,
sin broke into life : the Law was always an external,
compelling code which killed the will. But the man to
whom the new life was communicated was in a different
position. The handwriting in decrees which was over
against him disappeared : man had a new power given
him and the holy life was the result. He had no longer
to suppress and stifle his will in order to force it into
subjection to an external rule ; love, joy, and peace were
the natural and proper fruits of the Spirit which was in
him. They result because the Spirit is actually there ;
a definite change, a new inspiration have actually taken
place, and the virtuous life is the necessary consequence.

If we may put the same point in S. John's words, ' Every
' one that is born of God doeth no sin, because His seed
' abideth in him : and he cannot sin because he is born of
' God ' (1 John iii. 9). It is therefore a complete inversion
of the true purpose and significance of Christianity to
treat it as primarily a moral system or code. Codes as
such have disappeared. But that disappearance does not
mean licence to sin : ' God forbid ', says S. Paul, ' that we
should sin in order that grace may abound.' It is a
grotesque parody of Christianity to represent it as justi-
fying sin by appeal to higher laws, and tolerant outlooks,
and the contrast of letter and spirit, and all the para-
phernalia of much modern fiction : the gift of the Spirit
means union with God, and action such as this union will
produce. The carnal man will always find the spirit
much harder and more austere than the letter : he does
not receive the things of the Spirit of God ; they are
foolishness to him, and he cannot grasp them because
they are spiritually discerned. The man in whom the
Spirit dwells and abides will not fear austerity or sacrifice any more than Christ did, but he will look upon it with
the eye of the friend and not the slave, because he knows
what the Master doeth.

I have endeavoured to show that we have in Christianity a real and consistent way of looking at things,
which depends upon the relation of man and God, and
is governed throughout by this idea. I have also
endeavoured to show the real difference which this
character of the Christian attitude involves from the
philosophical way of looking at things. I must now
approach the very difficult question of the validity of the
Christian point of view.

Supposing some one arises and argues as follows :

I

'You have made a great distinction between a system of
'ideas, and a theology which bases itself on actual
'historical contact between the soul and God. Is this
'more than another idea? I grant you that if a man
'believes that he has the Spirit of a loving God within
'him he is more likely to be moved to action than he
'would be by the idea of the Absolute, or the abstract
'picturesqueness of self-sacrifice. But is the difference
'really more than a different way of putting things?
'You give an emotional, may I say an anthropomorphic,
'expression to what I call the Absolute: is there any
'more difference than this?'

I think that there are several things that should be said
on this point. In the first place, I doubt whether such
a question as is raised in the above assumed question
would have been intelligible to S. Paul or any of the
persons with whom he acted. He would, no doubt, have
believed, as you and I do in practice, that our ordinary
experience gives us access to the real world. The stripes
administered to him, in spite of his Roman citizenship,
at Philippi would have been as real to him as to you or
me. I do not suppose that the vision on the road to
Damascus would have been more or less real to him
than the highly unpleasant experience at Philippi. But
if you take a modern man he would probably say that,
though it may be hard to explain the reality of strokes
with rods on the bare back, these, at any rate, satisfy
certain criteria of reality, but a vision such as that on
the Damascus road does not. A medical man would
find evidence of the blows on the back, and could swear
to that effect in a law court; but the vision would leave
no traces behind it, and might be either fraud or delusion. Now, when the modern man says this, or anything
like this, he implies, consciously or unconsciously, that

nothing is *real*, nothing can be sworn to in evidence, except what may be expressed in terms of matter and motion. The marks on the back are evidence of beating.

I think that argument of this sort would greatly have astonished S. Paul. To his mind, and probably to the mind of all his fellow Christians, their intercourse with God was as real as their contact with the jailer at Philippi. Their scheme of the world included the presence and real contact with God: a vision might be a rare thing—a thing only vouchsafed to special people in special circumstances—but there could be no *a priori* reason for denying its possibility. If God exists, how can any one say that He cannot reveal Himself to any human soul, in any way He pleases?

Now all this means that between us and the early Christian mind there is a great division. On the whole, we assume a material world and look for evidence that can be expressed in terms of the world we know best. We endeavour to prove our spiritual facts as if they were facts of ordinary occurrence. We hope to rest a sound belief in immortality on the capacity of a medium to hammer out a quotation in Euripides. Our scheme of things is limited, consciously or unconsciously, by our physical environment, and we expect to deal with any conceivable experience in one way.

Secondly, I think it is becoming increasingly plain that this way of dealing with experience is abstract and one-sided. There is a vast range of our knowledge which can be covered by the methods of natural science: indeed, there is no part of it which is not, on one side, amenable to these processes. All thought and all speech have their physical side and are 'explicable' in scientific terms. But it is only the physical side that is thus explained. The meaning of the words, and their effect

on the mind, is not explained at all by their physical
accompaniments. From the physical side, there is little
difference in saying to a man ' It is a fine day ', or ' Your
house is on fire ', but there will probably be a great deal
of difference in his reaction to the two statements. The
physical side of these utterances is, as I have said, almost
the same ; but the difference in their result means that
the physical side of them is one-sided and abstract. If,
therefore, we insist, consciously or unconsciously, upon
physical tests for all kinds of reality, it means that we
are sure to be often wrong, and to reject much that is
true. I should contend, therefore, that it is unsafe to
rule out indiscriminately allegations which do not satisfy
certain tests. It may be possible to pass to the notion
of the Absolute from the simplest generalizations from
experience, but it is also possible that the process may
lead us farther from, instead of nearer to, reality.

I have contended several times in the course of these
lectures that the philosophical view of things fails to
explain the individual experience and the historical
sequence of events, all of which are individual. I submit
that the Christian scheme of thought, as it covers much
more ground, is able to avoid this pitfall. It has room
within it for the philosophical method, but it is not bound
within these limits. If the Christian point of view is to
be trusted the existence and activity of God is the
fundamental fact in experience. This fact, if true, must
express itself in contact with the souls of men, in the
general guidance of history, and the convergence of it on
a purpose, only partly fulfilled as yet. I have urged that
a sense of a presence in the world formed part of the
original reaction of man to his environment. There is
the same sort of reason for regarding this as true as
there is for trusting the effort towards intelligible order

and moral right. If I am right in my speculation upon this stage of things these various elements in man's view of the world were fused—did not exist as separate and possibly rival systems. They have been distinguished as experience grew, and as various aspects of it attracted various minds. But the religious impulse in its Christian form brings them all again into a kind of unity. God is not a mere presence in the world ; He has made it, guides its history in righteousness, strives to win the men in it, has loved and saved it. This is the thread which holds the whole system together, and every man has his own interest and part in it. In a sense, it is impossible to prove that this scheme of experience is valid, because it is impossible to get outside it. But I would contend that it cannot be invalidated, so to say, by the vote of the philosopher, whose view is so much more restricted, and who finds some factors in our experience so intract-able. Its claim to confidence rests upon its comprehen-siveness, that is, the wide range of its bearing on life and upon the verification which Christian experience constantly supplies. It gives significance to the individual acts which make up history, and finds them their place as such in the scheme. The sin or the self-sacrifice of this or that man is not merely one of a class of acts, nor can it be explained fully on general grounds. It is an un-changeable self-determination which takes the individual nearer to, or farther from, God, and goes towards the fulfilment of the whole Purpose of the world, whether or no the agent assents and consciously tries to forward God's aim. However deeply we penetrate into the secrets of nature, however great the control which the laws we discover give us over the forces of the world, its real meaning is the religious one, the response of the wills of men to the God who rules in righteousness.

IV

IN the last three lectures I have endeavoured to lead
up to the position that religion supplies a real and most
comprehensive view of all experience. It begins, as I
think, with a sense of a Being in the world, who works
in it in some fashion, and who is more approachable at
certain places and times, and by certain methods than
others. In this rather inarticulate conviction are hidden
the germs of science and philosophy, art and ethics, as
well as religion in its higher forms. The Greek mind
was primarily attracted by the philosophical idea of unity
in diversity, the effort to reconcile the one and the many :
the Hebrew mind was drawn rather towards the development of the religious idea. Owing to this divergence of
interest, two very different developments have taken
place. On the whole, the philosophical mind tends to
limit its operations to the region of ordinary experience ;
the religious mind tends always to look upon the course
of this world as serving a divine purpose wider than itself.
It is obvious that there must be a good many points upon
which the followers of these divergent views will not see
eye to eye. I propose in the present lecture to consider
some of these antagonisms.

I. There is a deep divergence as to the real nature of
the world-process. The Hebrew view of the world,
culminating in Christianity, rests upon the purposive
activities of a Divine Being, who created the world, as
we must express ourselves, in time, and rules it by means
of actions which again we must say, occur in time. There
is no phrase more fundamental to this point of view than

S. Paul's 'the fulness of the times'. The idea of Creation prevails, of course, very widely over the world ; it appears in many mythologies, and even Plato in the *Timaeus* (29 e–30 a) says of God—or τόδε τὸ πᾶν ὁ συνιστάς: ἀγαθὸς ἦν, ἀγαθῷ δὲ οὐδεὶς περὶ οὐδενὸς οὐδέποτε ἐγγίγνεται φθόνος· τούτου δ᾽ ἐκτὸς ὢν πάντα ὅτι μάλιστα ἐβουλήθη γένεσθαι παραπλήσια ἑαυτῷ. . . . βουληθεὶς ὁ θεὸς ἀγαθὰ μὲν πάντα, φλαῦρον δὲ μηδὲν εἶναι κατὰ δύναμιν, οὕτω δὴ πᾶν ὅσον ἦν ὁρατὸν παραλαβὼν οὐχ ἡσυχίαν ἄγον ἀλλὰ κινούμενον πλημμελῶς καὶ ἀτάκτως, εἰς τάξιν αὐτὸ ἤγαγεν ἐκ τῆς ἀταξίας, ἡγησάμενος ἐκεῖνο τούτου πάντως ἄμεινον. This is not, strictly speaking, a theory of creation, because the visible matter of the world is there already, in a state of confusion and disorder ; but God being incapable of envy brings order into it. And this is a characteristic of many creation myths : the deity is conceived not as making an absolute beginning, but as remodelling some material already in existence. This is, in reality, a very important difference, and it marks a profound divergence from the other point of view. The story we have in Genesis, which largely ruled Hebrew thought, certainly assumes an absolute beginning, but does not offer any explanation of it or give us any picture of the process. I will try to illustrate the effect of the difference.

(*a*) The notion of an absolute beginning is almost impossible to conceive in any relation with ordinary experience. The world is always there. When a man comes into it he finds it going on, and he has to put up with it : when his time draws near for leaving it, he overhears it, as it were, saying to itself : There are no necessary men. While he lives, all his thought and activity of every kind are in relation to it ; he can alter the position of material things and in various ways make them suit his convenience. He can put his wheel in such a relation to the stream that it will drive his mill. He can use his imagination and picture things not as they are but as he would like to have them. But in his loftiest efforts he flies very low and near the ground; he never gets outside the environment he came into when he was born, and he cannot picture a situation without the world, any more than he can conceive his own non-existence. He can *talk* of such things, because the gift of language enables us to use words without any positive meaning ; but that is all.

(*b*) But this is an unsatisfactory conclusion. The world, as man sees it and knows it, is a process of perpetual change. Moreover, the changes are not without rule or method. Man himself is guided in what he does by purpose or motive : is there something like this in the world ? Again, human action begins in time and occurs at a particular place and under particular conditions: when a man has made up his mind what he wants to do, he sets in motion various expedients for attaining it. Is there a parallel to this also in the world-order ? Can we think of it, or perhaps rather, can we help thinking of it as a process conveying a purpose, not a mere sequence of causes and effects, beginning nowhere and without definite end ? On lines like these men begin to try to prove the existence of God. They begin to talk of a First Cause, and trace the signs of purpose in the world around them. But so far back as Aristotle this was found to create difficulties. 'Is there any 'reason', he asks (*Phys.* ii. 8), 'why nature should not ' act without purpose, not for the better end, but as the ' sky (Zeus) rains, not to swell the corn, but of necessity. ' The vapour when drawn up *must* be cooled, and the

'cooled vapour *must* become water and fall. The fact
'that when this happens the corn grows is an accident
'(συμβαίνει). . . . So, is there any reason why the parts
'(of animals) should not be in the same position ; why it
'should not be a matter of necessity, for instance, that
'the front teeth grow sharp, suitable for cutting, and the
'molars are broad and useful for grinding the food—not
'to serve this purpose, but by accident?' Animals
unsuitably developed would die out. Aristotle does
not accept this view : a few lines farther down he says
action and nature are both for an end. If I may para-
phrase his language somewhat, it seems to come to this :
'According to function, so is structure, and according to
'structure so is function in each case, unless there be
'some disturbing factor. And function is purposive :
'structure therefore has the same end.'

(*c*) There is what philosophers call an antinomy—a
conflict between two tendencies of thought which look
equally persuasive. Man uses his powers in a certain
fashion, and it seems natural to him to construe the world
on similar principles. He is always trying to push over
the border of the ordinary experience, and reach out to
an active, deciding will. But there is always the doubt
whether he need do so : whether the exact statement of
sequences will not make all things plain. The metaphysical proofs of the existence of God are never convincing : it is hard to believe that all we think highest
in human activity should be the result of accident and
non-purposive combinations, but can we prove anything
else?

Much of this trouble arises from the fact that the
whole discussion arises within the limits of what we can
observe in the world around us. There used to be an

K

old problem, Which came first, the owl or the egg ? There is no answer to this question. It is not adequately stated. If the owl is granted, favourable circumstances may issue, not in an egg, but in an owl's egg ; if the owl's egg is granted, favourable circumstances may end in an owl.

But no amount of discussion at this stage will explain how the owl or the egg, whichever was first, got there. So long as we treat the world as a closed system of sequences, we may come from time to time to the edge and look wistfully over the boundaries, but we shall never get any farther. No amount of observation of the uniformities prevailing within the system will explain how the system got there.

But at this point in modern times a new question is raised. What of evolution ? Does not this theory get over the main difficulties of the absolute beginning ? May not the evolutionist assume not a complete owl or an owl's egg but something not exactly either but with the capacity of becoming either, and so going on yet farther ? In the old days, when the universe was thought of as a kind of immense Zoological Gardens, with all the creatures in it planted each in his separate cage, the owl and egg difficulty was a real one : you had to go outside the observed sequence of owl and egg, and settle, if possible, who put the owl or the egg into the gardens. But now does not the principle of evolution get you out of all these difficulties ? I am afraid I think not. I am not an anti-evolutionist. It is surely certain by now that no formal principle has ever been devised which brings more facts into order, or supplies a more comprehensive method of introducing rationality into the confused mass of details which make up direct experience. I have long been convinced that this principle, towards which many approximations have been made in the past, is a necessary means of interpreting phenomena in our present age.

But it has to be remembered that the formula itself is not always easy to interpret, and that, from the logical point of view, it is open to some of the difficulties once raised in regard to motion. It works admirably within a definite area, but difficulty always arises when the limits of the area are reached. Suppose, for instance, that there is a real fundamental difference between the process we call life and the movements of non-living matter, the principle of evolution will not explain the difference. Evolution may be and probably is the explanation, or at any rate a way of bringing into rational order, of the changing manifestations of life, but it does not explain the arrival of life, if that is really different from what was there before. It often seems that this difficulty would be got over if, instead of a vast gap such as was assumed in the days before evolution, you assume a vast number of small changes ; but this argument is really ineffective. The point is not the number of the changes but the character of them : and if between any of them there is a real and fundamental difference that cannot be explained as a different form of a reality that remains the same. Certain of the Gnostic systems of thought which troubled the Church in its early days were apt to get into this difficulty. They assumed an inexorable separation between the Divine Nature and all matter. They could not admit the possibility that God should have created a great, coarse, material world such as this : and they endeavoured to bridge the gap by a series of intermediary beings. It is obvious, of course,

that this expedient is a failure : the whole case is sur-
rendered if the Deity is permitted to make any step out
of the severe and isolated purity of his spiritual being.
It may be said that this line is mere logic—some might
even say logic-chopping. I am not concerned to deny
this : but I would urge that it is logic trying to secure
the self-consistency of a formula by which it is proposed
to interpret the world. But I would submit that evolution, like other formulae of interpretation and analysis,
is subject to the limitation, that you get out of it in the
end what you put into it at the beginning : or, in more
attractive language, it is a formula based upon and
applied to a certain selected series of phenomena, and
deals with a particular issue in regard to them. It
involves no criticism upon it if it proves inadequate to
issues other than this.

II. A second problem is concerned with the existence
of evil. Here again there is a divergence between the
Christian view of the world and that which arises from
observation of physical phenomena. To the Christian
mind, as I have pointed out in a previous lecture, evil is
in the end sin : i.e. rebellion by the finite will against
God. From the alternative point of view, evil, though
at times a deliberate form of wrongdoing, is not wrong
so much as imperfection, a mischief inherent in the
structure of creation. In ancient times the most natural
way of expressing this conviction would be to say that
evil is inherent in matter, or the world of sense. The
soul, conceived as an immaterial entity, suffered grievous
wrong by falling from its high estate and becoming
enveloped in a material body. The only hope for the
future lies in its deliverance from this bondage, and
restoration to the purity of its own natural life. Various

efforts were made to attach this belief to Christian doctrine. The Gnostic sects and the Manichaeans ultimately rested their theories upon the incompatibility of spiritual, and therefore of holy, life with any contact with matter. They offered schemes by which the soul should gradually be delivered from its imprisonment, and they used a certain amount of Christian language in order to set forth their ideas. The essential feature in them all is that evil is inherent in some way in the system of things, and not primarily in the will, and thus the process of overcoming it is, as it were, physical rather than moral. The soul requires separating from its corporeal bondage, not fundamental change in itself, and reconciliation to God.

In this connexion also the principle of evolution has been invoked to deal with the problem. It has been pointed out with perfect truth that man has in certain regions and under certain conditions raised himself to an almost unimaginable distance from the early state, through which it would appear that all races have passed. His moral ideas have developed in range and depth so that it is hard to recognize any unity of race between the educated European and the native of New Guinea. The whole development has occupied a comparatively short time, it would seem, in the history of the world, and there can hardly be any limit set to the hopes which may be realized in the future. All this is true, and it has been a misfortune that Christian writers and thinkers have underrated the value of the growth of civilization. The real criticism upon this method of dealing with the problem seems to me to be twofold. First, its main emphasis lies, in the end, on the outside of life mainly, on the discouragement and, perhaps, the disappearance of certain types of action. But this does not certainly imply a real change of will, and without this there is always danger of the reappearance of forms of evil which have been supposed obsolete. And, secondly, the plausibility cannot be denied of the view that the growth of civilization has not eliminated evil so much as changed its form. The civilized man does not do the same kind of wrongs as his savage brother; but he does others which are not less ruinous and cruel. We have got rid of the marauding Baron of the Middle Ages—we have reduced him to the state of being picturesque—but there are those who would say that the capitalist is much the same sort of thing : and though this view is not universally held, I suppose no one would deny that unscrupulous and self-regarding capitalism is of the same way of thinking as the marauding Baron, but has infinitely more capacity of wrongdoing. Surely no view of life ever received such a telling blow as the hope of eliminating evil by mere progress received in the late war. Growth in knowledge and mechanical skill, to which we owe most of our improved conditions of life, were used to make war more hideous than ever. It is true to say that all such things are morally indifferent, but to say that is the end of the hope that moral regeneration will come by their means.

III. I have spoken of two prominent differences between the two views of the world which I have brought to your notice. I want now to say a few words upon a question closely connected with these, but which is apt to arise in a rather different way. The view of the world which Christianity has developed on the basis of Judaism regards God as an active Sovereign over the world, guiding it through time to a purpose of which we know the nature only in part. What is the relation between the Divine Being, so conceived, and the world-order? Can He interfere with it at will? Can He, in short, work miracles? It always seems to me that this is a question of somewhat subsidiary interest in itself, though, of course, its connexion with New Testament criticism brings it into the region of popular discussion and controversy. To the ' man in the street ' the question means, Are the Gospels riddled with fictions? the real point at issue is, What do we think of God? If we think of God as simply a First Cause—a means of preventing an infinite regress of causation, or as the logical *prius* of a system of ideas based on observation of physical phenomena, then no doubt the question is at an end. God is so closely bound up with the world-order that the idea of variation is inconceivable. If, however, the relation of God to the world be conceived in a more personal form, the question of miracle is at least open to discussion. On this hypothesis the created order represents an act of purposive will on the part of God. He brings the world into being for a purpose and maintains it in existence. Unless the process is to be entirely haphazard, it will follow certain lines, all the more if it is to appeal to minds constructed as the minds of men are. There is nothing in this to exclude the possibility of variation from the order, if sufficient motive should arise ; because the laws, however rigid they might seem to us, have no independent or substantive existence of their own. That can only belong to them if there is nothing behind them, if the observed system of orderly sequences is the sum total of Being. If the existence and maintenance of the world depends upon the will of God, if at certain times, for example, He wished to attract the attention of men, or to make a new departure of any kind, it would be absurd to maintain that the rigidity of physical law bound Him.

Strictly speaking, I think, there is very little more to be said upon this question: there remains the problem of this or that alleged miracle, but that is for the historians, and cannot be dealt with by way of digression. There are, however, one or two points upon which a few words may be said.

(*a*) It is argued that there is a kind of essential impropriety in the idea that God can or would make any variation upon an order which He had sanctioned and set in motion. This runs back, probably, upon the rule laid down by Plato that God cannot change His will. S. Thomas Aquinas, in answer to this, points out that there is a difference between changing one's will and willing a change.[1] There is, however, a real issue involved in the problem. It is not possible to allow that the will of God is capricious or unstable, and it was to avoid this that Plato laid down his principle. It must be admitted that this point has been often overlooked, and it may be worth while to resuscitate for a few moments an old scholastic controversy, as it brings out the real point at issue. There was a difference of opinion between Thomas Aquinas and Duns Scotus on the relation of Reason and Will in the Divine Nature. Aquinas held that Reason was prior, Scotus that Reason was governed by Will. It might be supposed that there was no sense and no possibility of decision in such a discussion. In fact it contains a very important problem. If with Scotus we say that Will is prior this will mean that all law, physical or moral, depends upon an arbitrary determination. Murder, adultery, theft, are wrong because it is so

[1] *Summa*, pt. i, sec. 19, art. 7, corp. art.

ordered, and not for any inherent cause. On the principle
adopted by Aquinas this consequence is avoided, and a
better conception of truth and order attained : nature and
life to the Thomist are orderly because that is inherently
right, to the Scotist there is an inherent irrationality in
the whole scheme.[1] If therefore I contend that the
Christian view of God implies the possibility of what we
call miracle, I do so with the thought in my mind that
the miracle will never be arbitrary but will find its place
in the divine scheme.

This leads me to the second point I wish to touch upon
in this connexion. It is often argued that if a miracle
can be brought under any rational principle, it ceases at
once to be a miracle. It is true, of course, that if a
miracle is explicable in the sense that a conjuring-trick is
explicable, it ceases to have any quality that can reason-
ably be called miraculous. But it does not follow from
this that all miracles should be essentially irrational, and
have no place in any rational scheme of any kind. But
it is very widely assumed that there is a special virtue in
upsetting the existing order, and that unless that is done
there can be no real value in the act. Far the largest
number of alleged miracles proceed upon this hypothesis,
and that is one great reason why the whole subject is in
danger of becoming ridiculous. It is of interest in this
connexion to look at the Apocryphal Gospels and Acts :
there is no point in which they present a more remarkable
contrast to the Canonical Books than this one. The
miracles alleged to have occurred by the Canonical writers
are on the whole reserved in character, and involve little
disturbance of the natural order. They reveal a power,
always present, more definitely, but they leave the world

[1] Cf. Baur, *Lehre der Dreieinigkeit*, vol. ii, pp. 634 foll.

much as it is: when they seem likely to lead to misconception they do not occur. Whoever conceived them
had a great reverence for the order of the world. It is
wholly different with the non-canonical books, and it
must be remembered that these were written to satisfy
average expectations. The whole order of nature is
overthrown. In the *Protevangelium Iacobi* (which is
based upon our S. Matthew) we read that at the moment
of the birth of the Lord the whole process of nature
was suspended. Streams ceased to run: people at their
meals stopped with food on the way to their mouths: it is
like the story of the Sleeping Beauty. These books often
had considerable popularity, and were certainly more in-
teresting to certain types of mind. But the Church re-
jected them, its conception of nature and of history,
though unscientific enough in many ways, was better
than this.

I must now endeavour to put as clearly as I can the
general point I have had in view in these Lectures. I
suggest then that the world, if it is adequately conceived,
is a system made and controlled by God, and that this
view of it was present germinally at the very earliest
stage at which we can speak of a definitely human
reaction to the environment. This view of the world
contains elements which it is possible to distinguish and
treat in separation: moreover, they have been and are
usually treated in separation. In the Christian religion
they are brought into connexion again and recognized as
elements in a vast historic scheme. The reason why we
can say this of the Christian religion is that it rests upon
certain definite events occurring in history: a definite
movement on the part of God which throws light back-
ward on the past, interpreting its hopes and aspirations,

and also puts human life and its various interests in their proper relation. The Incarnation makes it possible to understand the relative order of man's ideas, and the real significance of his history : and it makes plain that the control, in spite of apparent failures, is in the hands of God.

Apart from some such scheme as this, I do not think it is possible to attain any really coherent conception of the world at all. All that is covered by the name religion is sure to prove a recalcitrant element in any scheme of things in which it is treated as a subordinate or secondary or derivative element. It can be made to look like a result of the analysis of outward experience, but I think, as I have already urged, that whenever that is done, it loses all its distinctive character, and turns into pantheism. And when this happens, the world becomes merely an inexplicable object, within which uniformities of various sorts can be traced, but which comes from nowhere, and goes nowhere. And this, I think, is in reality a completely irrational result. If any rational way is to be found of putting the world in connexion with religion, the distinctive features of religion must be present—in forms, no doubt, of growing definiteness and scope—from one end of the evolution to the other. The difference which Christianity makes to all this is, as I have just said, that for those who hold its tenets, many things which were mere ideas before have become assured facts. The historic process is a real process.

I will add, in conclusion, one or two remarks upon certain lines of possible criticism. It may be said, What do you make in your scheme of the enormous world of scientific research which covers more and more ground each year, and effects more profoundly all our life? I should answer that I do not propose to interfere with it, or limit it, or underrate it in any way. I do, however, venture to maintain that it is not concerned with all possible existence, but with a certain precise and definite field or aspect of existence. It deals with all that can be expressed in terms of matter and motion. But if there are things, as I think there are, which are not covered by those categories, then I should venture to question whether we shall arrive at truth by endeavouring to express them in those categories. There is, as it seems to me, a real distinction between the province of scientific research, and I would add of metaphysical speculation, and that of religion, and conflict is sure to arise if either party tries to deny the jurisdiction of the other. But I should add further, that though I think there is room within the historic conception of the world character- istic of Christianity for all that science and metaphysics can possibly claim, there is not room inside natural science and metaphysics for the claims of Christianity.

(*b*) It may be urged that one important school of thinkers at the present time is inclined to warn us against tying up our faith with historic events, and would endeavour to preserve the ideas which they are supposed to embody. Why trouble, for instance, about a physical resurrection, they would ask, if we have the notion of immortality secure? To this I would answer in brief that no one has ever succeeded, on the basis of argument, in making the idea of immortality secure, whereas the Resurrection, if it happened, not only clears up the meaning of immortality, but welds it into the whole system of actual experience. It seems to me that there is no less hopeful programme possible than that of dropping history and taking ideas as a substitute; it destroys the distinctive character of Christianity, and reduces it to a form of speculation. Christianity grips the whole historic order, and reveals ideas in the fertile and yet final form of definite acts and historic events.

Once more, it may be asked, How do you account for the fact that modern thought has given itself up so completely to the analysis of experience, and, if you are right, has misconceived the position of religion? If I may say what is in my mind, I think the reason goes back to the Renaissance—to the recovery of Greek learning—and the disparagement of all post-classical thought and writing. Most of us have a very discontinuous notion of the history of thought. We have begun, if we were wise, with Plato and Aristotle: some bold men have perhaps grappled with Plotinus. A rather larger number have groped in the grey and dingy atmosphere of Stoic Ethics. But a very large number of people, for instance, who read for the School of Literae Humaniores at Oxford pass straight from Plato and Aristotle to Descartes, Spinoza, Locke, Hume, Kant, and now, of course, modern psychology. In all these theology is a secondary product, it may be approached through the Proofs of the Existence of God, or in some such fashion: it is no part of the system of things. To persons trained in this fashion the whole line of Christian philosophers—Clement of Alexandria, Origen, Dionysius Areopagite, Augustine, Scotus Erigena, Peter Lombard, Anselm, Thomas Aquinas, Duns Scotus, Occam, Wycliffe, Raymundus Sebundensis—are scarcely even names. It is difficult to see what ought to be done: I fear it would be an unpopular proposal that all students of philosophy should be required to display a knowledge of patristic and scholastic philosophy: in Oxford just recently a

Professorship of the Philosophy of the Christian Religion
has been founded, and a distinguished Oxford philosopher
—Mr. C. C. J. Webb—has been appointed to it. I
do not offer any suggestions of this kind. But I do
express the opinion that the strangeness of a view of
things in which the main Christian principles are taken
in connexion with the subjects of other lines of discussion
is due to the way in which most of us approach the
problem, and not to inherent oddness in the view itself.
And I wish to leave with you my conviction that the
problems before us are not accurately stated if they are
raised within a limited and abstract section of experience,
and that the Christian faith not only restores proportion
and order to our idea of the world, and thereby helps us
to ask the right questions and so towards obtaining the
right answers, but it is the ideal form in which the deep-
seated impulse of man to seek after God is expressed
and satisfied.

www.ingramcontent.com/pod-product-compliance
Lightning Source LLC
Chambersburg PA
CBHW021425090426

42742CB00009B/1258